Achieving QTS
Reflective Reader: Primary English

Achieving QTS: Reflective Readers

Reflective Reader: Primary Professional Studies
Sue Kendall-Seatter
ISBN-13: 978 1 84445 033 6 ISBN-10: 1 84445 033 3

Reflective Reader: Secondary Professional Studies
Simon Hoult
ISBN-13: 978 1 84445 034 3 ISBN-10: 1 84445 034 1

Reflective Reader: Primary English
Andrew Lambirth
ISBN-13: 978 1 84445 035 0 ISBN-10: 1 84445 035 X

Reflective Reader: Primary Mathematics
Louise O'Sullivan, Andrew Harris, Margaret Sangster, Jon Wild, Gina Donaldson and
Gill Bottle
ISBN-13: 978 1 84445 036 7 ISBN-10: 1 84445 036 8

Reflective Reader: Primary Science
Judith Roden
ISBN-13: 978 1 84445 037 4 ISBN-10: 1 84445 037 6

Reflective Reader: Primary Special Educational Needs
Sue Soan
ISBN-13: 978 1 84445 038 1 ISBN-10: 1 84445 038 4

Achieving QTS

Reflective Reader
Primary English

Andrew Lambirth

Learning Matters

First published in 2005 by Learning Matters Ltd.

British Library Cataloguing in Publication Data
A CIP record for this book is available from the British Library.

ISBN-13: 978 1 84445 035 0
ISBN-10: 1 84445 035 X

Cover design by Topics – The Creative Partnerhsip
Project management by Deer Park Productions
Typeset by PDQ Typesetting Ltd
Printed and bound in Great Britain by Bell & Bain Ltd, Glasgow

Learning Matters Ltd
33 Southernhay East
Exeter EX1 1NX
Tel: 01392 215560
Email: info@learningmatters.co.uk
www.learningmatters.co.uk

Contents

Introduction

The series

The *Reflective Reader* series supports the *Achieving QTS* series by providing relevant and topical theory that underpins the reflective learning and practice of primary and secondary ITT trainees.

Each book includes extracts from classic and current publications and documents. These extracts are supported by analysis, pre- and post-reading activities, links to the QTS standards, a practical implications section, links to other titles in the *Achieving QTS* series and suggestions for further reading.

Integrating theory and practice, the *Reflective Reader* series is specifically designed to encourage trainees and practising teachers to develop the skill and habit of reflecting on their own practice, engaging with relevant theory and identify opportunities to apply theory to improve their teaching skills.

The process of educating individuals is broader than the specific areas of educational theory, research and practice. All humans are educated, socially, politically and culturally. In all but a few cases humans co-exist with other humans and are educated to do so. The position of an individual in society is determined by the nature and quality of the educational process. As a person grows up, emerging from childhood into adulthood, their social and political status is dependent on the educational process. For every task, from eating and sleeping to reading and writing, whether instinctive or learnt, the knowledge and experience gained through the process of education is critical. Humans are educated, consciously and subconsciously, from birth. Education is concerned with the development of individual autonomy, the understanding of which has been generated by educational, sociological, psychological and philosophical theories.

The position of the teacher in this context is ambivalent. In practice each teacher will have some knowledge of theory but may not have had the opportunity to engage with theories that can inform and improve their practice.

In this series, the emphasis is on theory. The authors guide the student to analyse practice within a theoretical framework provided by a range of texts. Through examining why we do what we do and how we do it the reader will be able to relate theory to practice. The series covers primary and secondary professional issues, subject areas and topics. There are also explicit links to Qualifying to Teach Standards (QTS) that will enable both trainees and teachers to improve and develop their subject knowledge.

Each book provides focused coverage of subjects and topics and each extract is accompanied by support material to help trainees and teachers to engage with the extract, draw out the implications for classroom practice and to develop as a reflective practitioner.

While the series is aimed principally at students, it will also be relevant to practitioners in the classroom and staffroom. Each book includes guidance, advice and examples on:

- the knowledge, understanding, theory and practice needed to achieve QTS status;
- how to relate knowledge, theory and practice to a course of study;
- self reflection and analysis through personal responses and reading alone;
- developing approaches to sharing views with colleagues and fellow students.

Readers will develop their skills in relating theory to practice through:

- preparatory reading;
- analysis;
- personal responses;
- practical implications and activities;
- further reading.

Primary English

This Reflective Reader provides an important contribution to your learning how to become an effective teacher of Primary English. The extracts have been chosen to challenge your thinking about teaching English. This book provides questions rather than answers: it sets thinking challenges and raises issues about the daily work of teaching children to become literate. It is hoped that, through the process of thought and debate with others on your course, you will be stimulated to develop a well-informed and critical approach to the teaching of Primary English. This will mean reading the work in this book critically, too. Examine what is said with care; enrich your own thinking with further reading before coming to firm conclusions.

This book is not to be read in isolation. The only way you will understand teaching and learning is through reading, debate with other colleagues – students, teachers and academics – and most importantly, through the dialogue you have with children. If you are reading this alone, without access to any of these resources, you will need to be pro-active and ensure that you have the full compliment of support. Good teaching requires both an engagement with educational theory and the means for practical application (Calderhead, 1994): the one is no good without the other. Beginning to be a teacher of English is only a start. To develop further you will subscribe to professional and academic organisations and the journals that they produce in order to keep abreast of new initiatives and research. You will join the culture of dynamic, reflective and creative Primary English teachers.

In addition to encouraging debate and further reading about theory and practice, this book also encourages you to read children's literature. At the start of each chapter I make suggestions of titles that I have enjoyed reading myself and reading to children. These are just a guide. I also recommend that you set yourself a target of reading at least 50 children's books by the end of your course. Immerse yourself in texts produced for children.

Throughout the book I also encourage readers to write. I urge you to become regular writers for pleasure. In doing so you will understand better the process involved, develop your own creative abilities and enjoy the rich experience writing can offer writers as well as readers. I believe that good teachers are artists and like all artists they need to find ways to engage creatively with a variety of relevant forms of artistic endeavour. These experiences will enrich your teaching.

This book will help you to:

- engage the issues at a theoretical level with reference to key texts in primary English;
- explore the teaching of English in the primary stage of education;
- reflect on your own principles and development as a teacher and consider how this impacts on your work in the classroom.

Each chapter is structured around the key reflective prompts what, why and how. Each prompt is linked to a short extract. You will:

- read a short analysis of the extract;
- provide a personal response;
- consider the practical implications;

and have links to:

- supporting reading;
- the QTS standards.

A note on extracts

Where possible, extracts are reproduced in full but of necessity many have had to be cut. References to other sources embedded within the extracts are not included in this book. Please refer to the extract source for full bibliographical information about any of these.

The author

Dr Andrew Lambirth is a Principal Lecturer in Education at Canterbury Christ Church University. He taught in primary schools in Peckham and Bermondsey before moving to higher education in 1996. Since then he has published widely in the field of primary English with special interests in children's literature, poetry, the teaching of writing, popular culture and the politics of literacy. Publications include: *Understanding Early Literacy* (Trentham), *Poetry Matters* (United Kingdom Reading Association), *Creative Activities For Plot, Character and Setting Ages 5-9, 7-9 and 9-11* (Scholastic), *Creativity and Writing: Developing Voice and Verve* (Routledge), *Planning Creative Literacy Lessons* (David Fulton).

Series editor

Professor Sonia Blandford is Pro-Vice Chancellor (Dean of Education) at Canterbury Christ Church University, one of the largest providers of initial teacher training and professional development in the United Kingdom. Following a successful career as a teacher in primary and secondary schools, Sonia has worked in higher education for nine years. She has acted as an education consultant to ministries of education in Eastern Europe, South America and South Africa and as an adviser to the European Commission, LEAs and schools. She co-leads the Teach First initiative. The author of a range of education management texts, she has a reputation for her straightforward approach to difficult issues. Her publications include: *Middle Management in Schools* (Pearson), *Resource Management in Schools* (Pearson), *Professional Development Manual* (Pearson), *School Discipline Manual* (Pearson), *Managing Special Educational Needs in Schools* (Sage), *Managing Discipline in Schools* (Routledge), *Managing Professional Development in Schools* (Routledge), *Financial Management in Schools* (Optimus), *Remodelling Schools: Workforce Reform* (Pearson) and *Sonia Blandford's Masterclass* (Sage).

Acknowledgements

Every effort has been made to trace the copyright holders and to obtain their permission for the use of copyright material. The publisher and author will gladly receive information enabling them to rectify any error or omission in subsequent editions.

The author and publisher would like to thank the following for permission to reproduce copyright material:

Barrs, M and Cork, V *The reader in the writer*, London, Centre for Literacy in Primary Education (2001). Reproduced with kind permission of Centre for Literacy in Primary Education, www.clpe.co.uk; Bearne, E, Dombey, H and Grainger, T (eds), *Classroom interactions in literacy*, Open University Press 2003. Reproduced with kind permission of the Open University Press/McGraw-Hill Publishing Company; Benton, M and Fox, G 'What happens when we read stories?' *Teaching literature 9–14*, OUP 1985. Reproduced with kind permission of Oxford University Press; Cordon, R *Literacy and learning through talk: Strategies for the primary classroom*, Open University Press, 2000. Reproduced with kind permission of the Open University Press/McGraw-Hill Publishing Company; D'Arcy, P *Two contrasting paradigms for the teaching and the assessment of writing: A critique of current approaches in the NC*, National Association of the Teachers of English (NATE) 2001. Reproduced with kind permission of NATE; Dombey, H 'Towards a balanced approach to phonics teaching' in *Reading,* vol. 33, no. 2, United Kingdom Reading Association. Reproduced with kind permission of Blackwell Publishing; Goodwin, P (ed), *The articulate classroom: talking and learning in the primary classroom*, David Fulton, 2001. Reproduced with kind permission of David Fulton Publishers. www.fultonpublishers.co.uk; Hall, K *Listening to Stephen read: Multiple perspectives on literacy*, Open University Press, 2003. Reproduced with kind permission of the Open University Press/McGraw-Hill Publishing Company; Hannon, P *Reflecting on literacy education*, Routledge, 2000.

Reproduced with kind permission of Taylor & Francis; HMSO, *Teaching talking and learning in Key Stage 2,* National Oracy Strategy. Reproduced with kind permission of HMSO; Kress, G *Before writing: Rethinking the paths to literacy,* Routledge, 1997. Reproduced with kind permission of Taylor & Francis; Lambirth, A (ed), *Planning creative literacy lessons,* David Fulton, 2005. Reproduced with kind permission of David Fulton Publishers. www.fultonpublishers.co.uk; Lambirth, A *Poetry matters* UKRA, 2002. Reproduced with kind permission of The United Kingdom Literacy Association; Medwell, J, Wray, D, Poulson, L and Fox, R, *Effective teachers of literacy,* Teacher Training Agency, 1998. Reproduced with kind permission of the Teacher Training Agency; Rosen, M, *Did I hear you write?* Five Leaves Publications, 1998. Reproduced with kind permission of Five Leaves Publications; Solar, J, Wearmouth, J and Reid, G (eds), *Contextualising difficulties in literacy development: Exploring politics, culture, ethnicity and ethics,* RoutledgeFalmer, 2002. Reproduced with kind permission of Taylor & Francis.

1   Learning a literacy

By the end of this chapter you will have considered:

- *why* schools teach the form of literacy they do;
- *what* it means to say there are multiple literacies;
- *how* teachers teach literacy most effectively and fairly.

Professional Standards for QTS
3.1.1, 3.3.2a, 6

Children's literature read:
Alan Durrant and Alan Riddell (1996), *Angus rides the goods train,* Viking.
What is the significance of this children's picture book to you? Are there any
contemporary issues for which you find the book particularly relevant?

Introduction

One of the aims of this *Reflective Reader* is to mirror the approach I want you to adopt
with the children in your class. I want to encourage a critical approach to your learning,
creating a dialogue between this book and you; you and the readings we offer; you
and your colleagues; and, eventually, you and your children. I hope this will construct
a truly professional perspective: to enable you to 'profess' about your work activities
and vocation.

The work presented in this chapter raises important questions about the nature of
literacy. In the first piece, Peter Hannon opens the debate on multiple literacies which
questions the wisdom and rationale of the present curriculum. The second piece
extends this argument by exploring the political dimensions involved in teaching particular forms of literacy to all children. In doing so, the authors suggest an alternative
paradigm for the teaching of English in schools and you are introduced to socio-
cultural perspectives for pedagogy which will be a regular theme throughout this book.

The third piece of work comes from a very influential research document that discusses
what 'effective' teachers of literacy do in their classrooms to promote high standards
of work.

The nature of literacy

One literacy or many?

Before you read the extract, read:
Chapter 1 of Gee (2004) *Situated language and learning.*

Extract: Hannon, P (2000) 'One literacy or many?', in *Reflecting on literacy education*. London: RoutledgeFalmer, pages 30–34.

The unitary view of literacy

Consider the following half-dozen quotations, taken from books about literacy. They are by authors with very different perspectives, and writing about different aspects of literacy, yet they all confidently refer to a single thing, 'literacy', which they assume readers will be able to recognise.

> By the learning of literacy, we mean the development of spoken language and written language from their origins in early infancy to their mastery as systems of representation for communication with others. (Garton and Pratt, 1998, p. 1)

> In the past 20 years, researchers and scholars working in early literacy have constructed a powerful knowledge base, concluding that children come to know literacy through their daily and mundane experiences in their particular social, cultural, religious, economic, linguistic, and literate societies. (Goodman, 1990, p. 115)

> To assess literacy properly, you need an objective definition of literacy for each age tested, up to and including adults. This means setting an absolute standard of literacy which is independent of the population's reading level, unlike standardized tests which simply reflect a population's ability. (McGuinness, 1998, p. 8)

> The success of a literacy campaign can only be fully evaluated in terms of its sustained impact. Too often people who pick up basic skills in well-publicized campaigns, lose those skills through disuse in the silent aftermath. Either no follow-up is available for consolidation, or the skills learnt find no applications. In rural areas, people who have spent their lives without the written word find little value in the techniques of reading and writing unless other aspects of their lives change. But if literacy is sustained it can provide the tools for people to make these changes themselves. (Archer and Costello, 1990, p. 33)

> The challenge in teaching literacy is to consider widely and appropriately a variety of perspectives, to provide the kind of balanced judgements which will best help the children in our care. (Beard, 1993, p. 3)

> Children create their literacy in contexts where: literacy is a meaningful event for them; where they see people participating in literacy for real purposes and with enjoyment; where people are prepared to discuss their literacy activities; where there are opportunities for children to participate in literacy; where child-initiated literacy behaviour is welcomed by adults; and where children's literate efforts are treated seriously. (Hall, 1987, p. 73)

Not only do these extracts unproblematically refer to 'literacy' as if everyone knows what it is but also they take it for granted that there is an 'it' which can be referred to. The 'it' is sometimes taken to be a skill or competence – the ability to use written language. According to this view the actual uses which particular readers and writers have for that competence is something which can be separated from the competence itself. It may be acknowledged that the uses depend on a complex of social, economic and political factors affecting the particular user of written language but it is suggested that the competence is intrinsically neutral.

The pluralist view of literacy

Despite its common sense appeal the unitary view of literacy presents some problems. The previous chapter showed that when literacy is viewed from an historical perspective, and when possibilities in the future are also contemplated, its nature is not so fixed. There are variations in the technology for mark making, in the conventions developed within different writing systems and in the uses for written language. If these can vary from one time to another, and also perhaps from one place to another, might the differences between variants be so great that what we are faced with is *different literacies* rather than different versions of a single thing called literacy?

One reason for taking this view is based on the fact that literacy is embedded in culture and since there are many cultures it could be argued that there are many literacies. This is not just a matter of variation in the particular written language or script being used or variation in subject matter. Of more significance can be variation in the *uses* of that written language. Even within countries such as Britain, the United States or Australia, and even among those inhabitants for whom English is a first language, there are different cultures and sub-cultures. They can be distinguished, for example, in terms of region, ethnicity, occupation, social class, gender and possibly social or institutional context. In each case the potential uses for written language may be the same but the pattern of actual uses may differ markedly. Writing for publication (in books or newspapers) is more common in middle class than in working class culture. Writing of personal letters may not vary so much. Reading of novels may well vary, but reading for information may not.

Two studies, among many, can illustrate how literacy is shaped by culture. In a classic study in the United States, Shirley Brice Heath (1983) has shown that *what* children learn at home about literacy can vary enormously according to the culture and values of their communities. She carried out a lengthy ethnographic study in the southern United States of two small neighbouring communities ('Trackton', black working class; 'Roadville', white working class) and found that their uses for literacy differed significantly from each other (and also from that of the 'mainstream' town community). For example, in 'Trackton', children were more likely to be involved in literacy events with several participants; in 'Roadville' bedtime stories were more common. Heath showed how these differences were rooted deep in culture and in patterns of oral language use. Despite having preschool literacy experiences, children from the two working class communities had difficulties with school literacy because their home literacies were not as congruent with the school literacy as was the case for the 'mainstream' community. The importance of this study goes far beyond what it tells us about literacy in the 1970s in two particular communities (which may no longer exist). It shows that children anywhere can learn about literacy before school, and out of school, but their literacy learning need not be the same. In a British study of older children Elaine Millard (1997) has shown how boys' and girls' uses of written language differ in terms of their choice of reading, their leisure activities and their preference for alternative forms of 'narrative distraction' such as television programmes, video recordings and computer games. The boys in Millard's study read fewer books and their preferred genres were not as congruent with school literacy (at least in terms of the English curriculum) as that of girls but in the long run Millard suggests that boys may be staking a claim to the more powerful, electronic forms of communication of the future. Although Millard does talk of boys and girls being 'differently literate', neither she nor Heath talk of different 'literacies'. Other writers, however, do discuss the issues in these terms.

Among theorists who contend that it is seriously misleading to use the word literacy when there are marked differences in what it means for different users in different contexts is Colin Lankshear (1987). He has challenged the unitary view as follows.

> There is no single, unitary referent for 'literacy'. Literacy is not the name for a finite technology, set of skills, or any other 'thing'. We should recognise, rather, that there are many specific literacies, each comprising an identifiable set of socially constructed practices based upon print and organised around beliefs about how the skills of reading and writing may or, perhaps, should be used.
> (Lankshear, 1987, p. 58)

David Barton (1994) has argued for a focus on what he terms 'literacy practices' – – common social practices associated with written language in a culture – and from this has argued for a pluralist view.

> Where these different practices cluster into coherent groups it is very useful to talk in terms of them as being *different literacies*. A literacy is a stable, coherent, identifiable configuration of practices such as *legal literacy*, or the literacy of specific workplaces.
> (Barton, 1994, p. 38, original italics)

James Gee (1996) argues that being able to read or write always means being able to read or write *something*, and, furthermore, if one examines specific instances, one finds that the way something is read or written always depends upon the reader's previous cultural experience of such texts.

> There are obviously many abilities here, each of them a type of literacy, one of a set of literacies. (Gee, 1996, p. 41)

Denny Taylor (1997) has put the case for recognising different literacies in the context of families' uses for written language.

> Descriptive studies of families and literacy in many different countries with many different cultural traditions have changed narrow preconceptions. These studies show that each family is an original, that there is a seemingly infinite variety of patterns of cooperation and domestic organization, and that flexible household arrangements are often an adaptive response to an uncertain world. Within family settings there are both multiple literacies and multiple literacy practices. (Taylor, 1997, p. 1)

David Barton and Mary Hamilton (1998) made use of the idea of different literacies in their detailed ethnographic study of literacy practices in one town in England.

> Looking at different literacy events it is clear that literacy is not the same in all contexts; rather, there are different literacies … within a given culture, there are different literacies associated with different domains of life. Contemporary life can be analysed in a simple way into domains of activity, such as home, school, work-place. (Barton and Hamilton, 1998, p. 9)

One consequence of 'seeing' different literacies is that it focuses attention on ways in which 'school literacy' may differ from, and may even be in conflict with, 'home literacy', 'community literacy' or 'workplace literacy'. For some families – specifically middle-class ones – there may be a high degree of congruence between home literacy, school literacy and workplace literacy but for other families school literacy may be far removed from that which they encounter at home or at work. This makes problematic the issue of whether some literacies can be regarded as more valuable than others (where literacy is viewed as unitary this issue tends to be hidden). In particular it forces a rethinking of the importance to be given to 'school literacy'.

Taylor (1997) suggests that what is sometimes seen as people's lack of literacy is actually them having the 'wrong' literacy, i.e. a literacy different from the dominant ones.

> Some of these literacies have become powerful and dominant, while others have been constrained and devalued. The problem is not so much a lack of literacy, but a lack of social justice. Local knowledge is not always appreciated and local literacies are not always recognized. (Taylor, 1997, p. 4)

Street (1984) has distinguished what he terms 'autonomous' and 'ideological' models of literacy. The 'autonomous' model embodies assumptions often made by educators and psychologists (that literacy alone provides certain cognitive benefits, that its development is unidirectional, that it is separable from schooling, and that it brings about economic, social and political progress). Street argues that this model over-generalises from one narrow, culture-specific literacy practice.

Also associated with the pluralist view is a rejection of the idea of literacy as a neutral skill. Lankshear (1987) has criticised the idea in these terms:

> I argue that literacy is the uses to which it is put and the conceptions which shape and reflect its actual use. Once this is admitted we do more than merely achieve relief from the gross reification of literacy involved in the literacy-as-a-neutral-skill-or-technology view. In addition, we are freed to ask a whole range of questions that we are effectively discouraged from asking if we assume that literacy is neutral. For we can now entertain the possibility that the forms reading and writing take in daily life are related to the wider operation of power and patterns of interest within society. (Lankshear, 1987, p. 50)

Gee (1996) has argued in a similar vein:

> the traditional view of literacy as the ability to read and write rips literacy out of its sociocultural contexts and treats it as an asocial cognitive skill with little or nothing

to do with human relationships. It cloaks literacy's connections to power, to social identity, and to ideologies, often in the service of privileging certain types of literacies and certain types of people. (Gee, 1996, p. 46)

Analysis

There has tended to be an assumption that literacy is a phenomenon that is unvarying and unitary in nature. This perspective conceptualised literacy as an autonomous set of technical skills that can be learned and then practised. However, there is now a growing tendency to regard literacy as a social practice that is bonded to ideology, culture, knowledge and power. This organic view of literacy sees it as a cultural activity defined by its cultural context and utilised according to the needs of a particular social community. As a consequence, literacy is now being regarded, not as one set of practices, but as many. There are indeed 'multi-literacies' suited to the range of context-related environments that exist.

Different homes and environments from different cultures formed by environment, ethnicity and even profession tend to use words in different ways. Research completed in the United States of America in the 1980s (Brice Heath, 1983) showed how culture influences literacy. Many of the children you will teach will come from homes that favour televisual texts rather than the printed word in order to access story narrative or information. Many will utilise oral communication rather than the printed word and/or they will practise complex literacy activities using religious texts in English or another language. You will need to be aware of the different home literacy practices and build upon them and tailor your teaching to engage children's attention and reveal the relevance of school literacy.

It can be argued that the National Literacy Strategy (DfEE, 1998) presents a package of literacy skills as if the concept of literacy were politically and ideologically neutral – that certain values and assumptions can not be discerned from what is stated as essential to learn. However, as the first reading in this chapter has illustrated, there are serious differences between the view of literacy as a collection of skills that should be delivered and learned by children and the perspective that sees literacy as a social practice. A teacher needs to consider and reflect upon how perspectives about literacy will affect the teaching and learning in the classroom. If we conclude that there are indeed different forms of literacy found in different social and ethnic groups, questions begin to arise concerning the nature of school literacy found in curricula.

- What are the criteria for choosing the distinct form of literacy found in curricula?
- Does the literacy curriculum advantage certain social groups who share the school form of literacy at home and disadvantage those who have different home literacies?
- Will learning school forms of literacy empower our children?
- Are there ways to build upon the forms of literacy with which children arrive in school in order to teach school literacy?
- Should this influence the way we assess children's literacy learning?

As Peter Hannon goes on to say, there is something rather unsettling about the notion that there are many literacies and not just one. It presents many questions about equality of opportunity, power and politics. For example, from which social group do the authors of the literacy curriculum derive? Are we happy that their values are the 'right' ones?

Personal response

- Discuss with a colleague your own literacy background. Was print literacy the majority form of literacy with which you grew up? Was the reading of books modelled for you as a child by your parents? Do the values that exist in your literacy background match the values behind school literacy?
- Is print literacy an important part of your leisure-time pursuits today?
- Do you believe certain forms of literacy practice are better than others? What do you base your opinion upon? Discuss this with a group of colleagues to compare views. Ask them if teachers should impose school literacy upon those who are content to use their own 'ways with words'.
- Discuss whether your colleagues think it is fair and inclusive that success and academic ability are based upon one's aptitude for a particular form of literacy. Does it help to explain underachievement or disaffection in some schools?

Practical implications and activities

The National Literacy Strategy *Framework for teaching* (DfEE, 1998) states with a robust certainty what literacy teaching needs to promote.

Literate primary pupils should:

- *Read and write with confidence, fluency and understanding;*
- *Be able to orchestrate a full range of reading cues (phonic, graphic, syntactic, contextual) to monitor their reading and correct their own mistakes;*
- *Understand the sound and spelling system and use this to read and spell accurately;*
- *Have fluent and legible handwriting;*
- *Have an interest in words and their meanings and a growing vocabulary;*
- *Know, understand and be able to write in a range of genres in fiction, poetry, and understand and be familiar with some of the ways in which narratives are structured through basic literacy ideas of setting, character and plot;*
- *Understand, use and be able to write a range of non-fiction texts;*
- *Plan, draft, revise and edit their own writing;*
- *Have a suitable technical vocabulary through which to understand and discuss their reading and writing;*
- *Be interested in books, read with enjoyment and evaluate and justify preferences;*
- *Through reading and writing, develop their powers of imagination, inventiveness and critical awareness.* (DfEE, 1998, p3)

Do you think that this form of literacy reflects the outside literacy world? Do you think it should?

What forms of texts are valued in this curriculum?

Which ones are ignored?

Why do you think they are?

Will this form of literacy interest and engage all children equally?

New times! Old ways?

Before you read the next extract, read:

- Hannon (2000) 'Literacy is fundamental', in *Reflecting on literacy education.*

Extract: Lankshear, C and Knobel, M (2002) 'New times! Old ways?', in Solar, J, Wearmouth, J and Reid, G (eds) *Contextualising difficulties in literacy development: Exploring politics, culture, ethnicity and ethics.* **London: RoutledgeFalmer, pages 266– 70, 276–82.**

Background

During recent years governments otherwise concerned with trimming public sector spending have often trumpeted 'funding packages' dedicated to improving 'literacy competence' among school-age and adult populations. Whenever such packages are announced, our own immediate response has increasingly been to wonder 'what does this package *really* mean so far as promoting a more literate and educated public is concerned?'

One of the authors recalls that during his final year of high school, in the context of a lesson on political reform in Britain, the history teacher made a link between three events and a political pronouncement. The events were the 1867 Reform Act (which extended the vote to some 1 million artisans living in the towns), the 1870 Education Act (which established a universal system of elementary schools for working-class children), and the 1884 Reform Act (which extended the vote to many 'unskilled' workers). The political pronouncement in question derived from Robert Lowe (Viscount Sherbrook), a champion of what became the 1870 Education Act. As interpreted by the history teacher, Lowe/Sherbrook was overtly advocating that a link be institutionalised between compulsory education, social control and economic interests. In other words: now that they are being given the vote, 'We must educate our masters.' The history teacher was, of course, far from alone in this interpretation. It has been almost a standard position among Marxist historians of British working-class education, notably Brian Simon (1960).

Lowe's views repay closer attention. In his letters and other written works, Lowe argued that, since they were the majority of the voting population, working-class males would have the numerical potential to become:

> masters of the situation [with the power] to subvert the existing order of things, and
> to transfer power from the hands of property and intelligence, and so to place it in

the hands of men whose whole life is necessarily occupied in the daily struggle for existence. ... I believe it will be absolutely necessary to compel our future masters to learn their letters. (Martin, 1893: 262; Simon, 1960: 354)

At the same time, the higher classes would need 'superior education and superior cultivation', in order to 'know the things the working men know, only know them infinitely better in their principles and in their details'. By this means the higher classes could 'conquer back by means of a wider and more enlightened cultivation some of the influence which they have lost by political change' (Lowe, 1867: 8–10; Simon, 1960: 356).

Given the benefits of such historically informed hindsight, it makes good sense to begin from the assumption that compulsory mass schooling probably has a lot less to do with *educating* and *making literate* (in any truly expansive sense of these terms) than it has to do with producing other outcomes: outcomes which we should strive to make clear, and for which we should call governments, education officials, and teacher educators to account. We should train ourselves to recognise evidence for this assumption when we see it – which is often.

We will proceed from this assumption here and try to turn some everyday assumptions upside down. Our aim is to expose some anomalies and contradictions, and to assess some high profile trends apparent within literacy education at present against criteria that do not (in our view) figure sufficiently in public and political debate around education.

Two questions: Wayne O'Neil (1970)
In a powerful short polemic, 'Properly literate', Wayne O'Neil prompts us to rethink some 'common sense' assumptions about (il)literacy and disadvantage.

Who's disadvantaged?
O'Neil says:

> I have known but two illiterate adult Americans.... One was an ancient, a Mr Cole, North Carolina potter of a line of North Carolina–Staffordshire, English potters as far back as memory reaches. He runs a prospering pottery shop on Route 1 just outside Sanford, NC. He finishes a firing every two weeks, everything gone long before the next firing is out of the kiln. People come in and order pots of all sizes and shapes and he has them write their orders in a fat, black book. Too bad. He can't read. They never get their pots. So they learn to buy what he has or leave a picture behind and then get back before someone else buys it.

> He does well. (O'Neill, 1970: 261)

Who's literate?
According to O'Neil:

> In the tangled, demanding revolution that is America, if you're illiterate you have no control or at most you have only narrowly limited control. If you can only read and remain illiterate, you're worse off: you have no control.

> Make a distinction: Being able to read means that you can follow words across a page, getting generally what's superficially there. Being literate means you can bring your knowledge and your experience to bear on what passes before you. Let us call the latter proper literacy; the former improper. You don't need to be able to read to be properly literate. Only in America and such like. (ibid.: 261–2)

O'Neil believes children arrive at school properly literate relative to their experience, even though many (if not most) do not yet read and write. In teaching them to read and write, however, schools undermine and undo that proper literacy. The ways of school instruction displace bringing knowledge and experience to bear on what passes before one. In its place they impose the following of mere words – whose words?, which words? – across printed surfaces. O'Neil rejects this 'usurper literacy', calling it *improper*. This, however, is precisely what Robert Lowe wanted from mass schooling; an 'antidote' to the highly effective political organisation and agitation working people had engaged in throughout the nineteenth century. The organised political practices of the working classes were, indeed, grounded firmly in 'bringing knowledge and experience to bear on what passed before them' – every day.

There are good reasons for believing that, collectively, we are doing a pretty good job in education of keeping faith with the Viscount. Peter Freebody's (1992) account of what counts as being a successful reader, given the everyday demands of our cultural milieu, provides a good starting point for our argument.

Four roles as a literacy learner

Freebody argues that to become a successful reader an individual must 'develop and sustain the resources to play four related roles: code breaker, text-participant, text-user, and text-analyst' (1992: 48).

1. Code breaker: This is a matter of cracking alphabetic code/script – understanding the relationship between the twenty-six alphabetic written symbols and the forty-four sounds in English, and being able to move between sound and script in reading/decoding and writing/encoding.

2. Text-participant: This involves being able to handle the meaning and structure of texts, by bringing to the text itself the additional knowledge required for making meaning from that text – for example, knowledge of the topic, the kind of situation involved, the genre of the text, etc. Mere ability to decode is not sufficient for making meaning from a text: we can read plenty where we cannot understand, or that we understand differently from other successful decoders. Much depends on what we bring to the text with us. When we are faced with texts that we cannot bring much to, or where we cannot bring what others (who are deemed to comprehend better than we do) bring, we are disadvantaged by, or in relation to, that text and other readers.

3. Text-user: Successful reading requires ability to operate effectively and appropriately in text-mediated social activities. According to Freebody (1992: 53), being a successful text-user 'entails developing and maintaining resources for participating in "what this text is for, here and now" '. Reading, then, is a matter of matching texts to contexts, and knowing *how*, *what* and *why* to read and write within given

contexts. It is what we sometimes refer to as getting the register or, perhaps, the genre 'right'. To foreshadow a theme we will return to later, Freebody comments that these resources 'are transmitted and developed in our society largely in instructional contexts, some of which may bear comparatively little relevance to the ways in which texts need to be used in out-of-school contexts' (ibid.).

4. Text-analyst: The reader as competent text-analyst is consciously aware that 'language and idea systems' are 'brought into play' whenever a text is constructed and, furthermore, that these systems are what 'make the text operate' and, thereby, make the reader, 'usually covertly, into its [i.e., the text's] operator' (ibid.: 56). Readers, in other words, become complicit in the work that texts do. This makes it very important to be aware of the need to interrogate texts, and to know how to interrogate them – since otherwise we may unwittingly participate in producing or maintaining, effects we would not knowingly choose to. As basic examples of text interrogation, Freebody suggests asking 'What are the beliefs about the topic of a person who could utter this text?', and, 'What kind of person could unproblematically and acceptingly understand such a text?' This can be pushed further, by asking what kind of world – as lived contexts and sites which shape human identities and ways of being – do such and such texts sanction, promote, bolster and implicate us in making and maintaining?

Freebody concludes by insisting that these four roles not be seen as some kind of a sequence – developmental or otherwise. Rather, they are jointly necessary conditions for being a successful reader. Hence, they are necessary components of being a reader at each and every phase of our development and practice as readers. Whatever students' ages or developmental points, their reading programmes must promote and deal with each role in systematic and explicit ways (ibid.: 58).

A sociocultural approach to literacies[1]

When we take a sociocultural approach to literacy we turn our attention from the mind and, ultimately, the school, and enter instead the *world*, including the adult world of work. From a sociocultural approach, the focus of learning and education is not *children*, nor *schools*, but, rather, *human lives* as *trajectories* through multiple *social practices* in various social institutions. If learning is to be efficacious, then what a child or adult does *now* as a 'learner' must be connected in meaningful and motivating ways with 'mature' ('insider') versions of related social practices.

The focus of education should be on *social practices* and their connections across various social and cultural sites and institutions. Learners should be viewed as life-long *trajectories* through these sites and institutions, as *stories* with multiple twists and turns. What we say about their beginnings should be shaped by what we intend to say about their middles and ends, and vice-versa. As *their* stories are rapidly and radically changing, we need to change *our* stories about skills, learning, and knowledge. Our focus, as well, should be on multiple learning sites and their rich and complex interconnections.

If learning is not to be a senseless activity (which, regrettably it sometimes is), it is always about entry into and participation in a Discourse.[2] Unfortunately, a focus on children and schooling tends to obscure the role of social practices and Discourses. Some Discourses, like law, have a separate domain for (initial) initiation into the Discourse (namely, law school). Others, including many Discourses connected to workplaces, do not engage in such a separation to any such extent. In these cases, much learning and initiation into the Discourse occurs 'on the job'. In both cases, however, the connection between learning and participation in the 'mature' Discourse (law or work) is relatively clear. The same is true of family, community and public sphere-based Discourses.

School-based Discourses are quite anomalous in this respect. Schools don't merely separate learning from participation in 'mature' Discourses: they actually render the connections entirely mysterious (as we will see in some cases provided below). Schools and classrooms most certainly create Discourses, that is, they create social practices that integrate people, deeds, values, beliefs, words, tools, objects and places. They create, as well, social positions (identities) for kinds of students and teachers. However, the discourse of the school or classroom is primarily a Discourse devoted to learning – but, learning for *what*? Is it learning for participation in the school or classroom Discourse itself, or learning for Discourses outside school? Which Discourses outside of school? And what sort of relationship to these outside Discourses should (or do) school and classroom Discourses contract?

These are complex questions and issues. The separation between school-based Discourses and 'outside' Discourses may be a good thing, or it may not be. It all depends on how we answer such questions as 'What is the point (goal, purpose, vision) of school-based Discourses?' 'What is the point (goal, purpose, vision) of this or that specific school-based Discourse (e.g., elementary school reading or secondary school English)?' What we *can* say, without much doubt, is that turning school Discourses of literacy into so many intervention programmes that undermine apprenticeship to 'mature' versions of social practices does no one much good in the long run. Neither does turning literacy into distinctively *school* Discourses. For evidence of this, let us turn, finally, to some real-life cases from local research.

Right now we are at an important literacy conjuncture. New literacy practices are emerging around new technologies which are making ever deeper incursions into everyday social practices, spanning the range from leisure to work, via communications, business, trade, etc. These changes have major implications for literacy learning, forcing us to consider what is involved in being a text-participant, text-user, and text-analyst in 'new times'. The cases which follow are intended to provide some insights into how different learners and teachers are negotiating the present conjuncture. They are based on fieldwork done in Queensland school, home and community settings (cf. Knobel, 1997), and have been further described in other publications (see Knobel, 1996; Lankshear and Knobel, 1996a, 1996b, 1997).

Critical social literacy as a millennium literacy
There are some ironies here. First, if we accept that education is about preparing people for the society they will enter, what we are currently doing in the way of literacy education may work just fine – as it has since the time of Robert Lowe. We can continue to develop and even enhance the capacity of people to break codes, participate in text-

mediated social practices, and use the normal range of texts – and take our chances on the shrinking range of pathways to viable and dignified futures, and all that goes with it: from escalating views among youth that there is no future; escalating rates of youth suicide; and escalating enactments of desperation. If nothing else, that may create jobs in property-guarding and personal security and the like. Schools can continue to generate established patterns of 'success' and 'failure', and to legitimate these through school Discourses and forms of assessment that deliver up league tables of 'good' schools and 'bad' schools, and that continue to generate interventions that focus on enhanced code breaking performances that are effectively roads to nowhere – or nowhere much. Equally, we can place our faith in high-tech classrooms that permit similar outcomes to be achieved with still larger class sizes – albeit with more alienating work conditions and lower remuneration rates for teachers, together with continuing experience of being blamed for the alleged consequences of a failing school system.

Alternatively, we can embrace a second irony: namely, that the literacies we need for the new millennium contain elements that have been practised and refined for thousands of years – as well as containing elements that are distinctively new. The call to interrogate texts critically in search of the good life is, in the Western tradition, at least as old as Socrates; and in other traditions as old if not older again. The call to create and engage texts which search for ways of actualising humanity on just and reciprocal bases is absolutely fundamental and binding to the 'post-everything' age. What we need to do as literacy educators is to reinvent textual practices that enable us to bring our knowledge and experience to bear on what passes before us, filtered through an ideal of lives of dignity and fulfilment for all, and grounded in a conviction that a world in which this ideal is possible remains open to people prepared to collaborate in building it. This is much more than a matter of being able to 'follow words across a page [or a screen], getting generally what's superficially there' – although for some time to come it will probably *include* the capacity to decode and encode print.

We do well to remember this when we look at multimillion dollar budget breaks for literacy. And we do well to remember also that much of what we need to consider is *already* available to us. It is, for example, available in concepts like C. Wright Mills' notion of 'sociological imagination' (Mills, 1959), when suitably reworked to take account of recent developments in social, ethical and epistemological theories advanced in response to distinctive conditions of lived experience in new times. It is also, we venture, available in a sociocultural approach to literacy which insists that language and literacy must always be understood in their social, cultural and political contexts. One of these contexts is the globally interconnected space of the new global economy, with its new competition and its new work order, *and in all its ramifications*. For

> language – indeed, our very humanity – is in danger of losing meaning if we do not carefully reflect on this context and its attempts to make us into 'new kinds' of people … e.g., people who are 'smart' because they [produce and] buy the highest 'quality' [with the greatest efficiency, accountability, and cost effectiveness], but do not care about – or even see – the legacies of their greed writ large on the world. (Gee, Hull and Lankshear, 1996: 150–1)

Endword

In the end, we have more to recover than our *reading*, although we have *that* to recover as well: albeit in a much more generous and expansive sense than many of our current practices admit – including some of those most in favour among politicians and administrators at present.

Notes

1   This section draws directly on Gee, Hull and Lankshear, 1996: 4, 6, 15–16.

2   In what follows we observe James Paul Gee's distinction between 'Discourse' and 'discourse'. For Gee, a Discourse is a 'socially accepted association among ways of using language, other symbolic expressions, and artefacts, of thinking, feeling, believing, valuing and acting that can be used to identify us as a member of a socially meaningful group' (Gee, 1991: 131). Gee uses 'discourse' to refer to the 'language bits' in Discourses: that is, connected stretches of language that make sense within some Discourse community or other (e.g., a report within a research Discourse), an essay within a scholastic Discourse.

Analysis

Welcome to the political world of education! As I discussed in the introduction to this book, many of the extracts you will read here present an opinion. It is the intention of this book to encourage you to rigorously engage and challenge the arguments that are presented before forming your own conclusions. The readings in this book raise issues that problematise areas one might assume are not contentious. Once again I hope this mirrors what you attempt to do with your children throughout the primary phase.

Lankshear and Knobel's piece raises some important issues and introduces some interesting concepts. When you begin teaching you will see how politics and education are intrinsically linked. This extract attempts to show the political and economic incentives for presenting certain forms of literacy in schools. The authors suggest that certain literacy curricula – 'improper literacy' – actually work against particular social groups, and 'education' becomes inhibitive rather than emancipatory. Lankshear and Knobel contend that some literacy teaching constructs the learners as passive recipients of skills, tailored primarily for the world of work, and they suggest, through Freebody's (1992) 'four roles' of a literacy learner, a way of creating active and powerful literacy users for life. In this model I want you to note the stress that Freebody puts on the need *not* to teach the components of literacy as a sequence, but always to teach all of the components all the time throughout children's school life. To be an effective, independent literacy user it is important that learners have all four roles.

The authors, elsewhere in this piece (not included here), attack teaching intervention strategies for reading and writing which concentrate on only the technical aspects of literacy learning, focusing on the code-breaking skills at the expense of other crucial components. They also condemn methods that teach about literacy that use decontextualised examples and ignore the uses of literacy in real-life situations. Indeed, the need to relate school learning to the real world and the social practices that go on there is what they mean by 'socio-cultural' approach. This means opening the classroom discourse to include new modes of communication, and the examples they give disclose the changing ways young people use literacy.

By contemplating these arguments you will begin to construct your own professional position on literacy teaching and will be able to make important decisions about how literacy will be taught in your classroom and school.

Personal response

- Discuss this extract with a colleague. One of you should adopt the role of an employer and one of you, an educator. What does the employer want from a literacy curriculum that would help the business s/he runs? What will the educator make of this perspective? Is this the curriculum s/he believes is right for the individual in society?
- Once you have discussed this as a pair, 'snowball' into a group of four, keeping your roles. Once you have discussed for a while, 'snowball' your group into a six.

Practical implications and activities

Discuss a literacy lesson that you have taught. Have your plan and your evaluation with you. Examine the Freebody model of the 'four roles' of a literacy user and identify the roles you were encouraging in your lesson.

For example:

- Did you encourage any texts that would be more familiar at home rather than school?
- Were there opportunities for the children to interrogate a text of any kind?
- Were they able to talk about their preferences and dislikes concerning the texts?
- Was there emphasis on any one of the roles?

Look at the intervention programmes provided by the National Literacy Strategy. Analyse them in terms of the balance they provide for the roles of the literacy user.

Effective teachers of literacy

Before you read this next extract, read:
Twiselton, S 'Beyond the curriculum: Learning to teach primary literacy', in Bearne *et al.* (2003) *Classroom interactions in literacy.*

Extract: Medwell, J, Wray, D, Poulson, L and Fox, R (1998) Chapter 8 in *Effective teachers of literacy: A report of a research project commissioned by the Teacher Training Agency*, pages 77–8.

8.3 The belief systems of effective teachers of literacy
- The effective teachers of literacy tended to place a high value upon communication and composition in their views about the teaching of reading and writing: that is,

they believed that the creation of meaning in literacy was fundamental. They were more coherent in their belief systems about the teaching of literacy and tended to favour teaching activities which explicitly emphasised the deriving and creating of meaning. In much of their teaching they were at pains to stress to pupils the purposes and functions of reading and writing tasks.

- Although they emphasised purpose and meaning in their belief statements, this did not mean that the more technical aspects of reading and writing processes were neglected. There was plenty of evidence that such aspects as phonic knowledge, spelling, grammatical knowledge and punctuation were prominent in the teaching of effective teachers of literacy. Technical aspects of literacy tended, however, to be approached in quite different ways by the effective teachers than by most of the teachers in the validation sample.

- The key difference in approach was in the effective teachers' emphasis on embedding attention to word and sentence level aspects of reading and writing within whole text activities which were both meaningful and explained clearly to pupils. Teachers in the validation sample were more likely to teach technical features as discrete skills for their own sakes, and did not necessarily ensure that pupils understood the wider purpose of such skills in reading and writing.

- Our finding concerning the beliefs of this group of effective teachers of literacy, that they prioritised the creation of meaning in their literacy teaching, thus reflects not that they failed to emphasise such skills as phonics, spelling, grammar etc. but rather that they were trying very hard to ensure that such skills were developed in children with a clear eye to the children's awareness of their importance and function.

8.4 The teaching practices of effective teachers of literacy

- There were some differences between the reading activities likely to be employed by the effective teachers and the teachers in the validation group. The effective teachers made more use of big books in their teaching; they were also more likely to use other adults to assist their classroom work. The validation teachers made more use of phonic exercises and flashcards, although both groups were similar in the extent to which they reported and were observed to teach letter sounds. The difference was in the ways they went about this. The effective teachers tended to teach letter sounds within the context of using a text (often a big book) and to use short, regular teaching sessions, often involving them modelling to the children how sounds worked (by, for example, writing examples of letter groups on a flip-chart). The validation teachers were much more likely to approach letter sound teaching through the use of paper exercises.

- The effective teachers were generally much more likely to embed their teaching of reading into a wider context and to show how specific aspects of reading and writing contribute to communication. They tended to use whole texts as the basis from which to teach skills such as vocabulary, word attack and recognition and use of text features. They were also very clear about their purposes for using such texts.

- In lessons involving writing the differences between the two groups of teachers were less clear although it did seem that the effective teachers were more likely to use published teaching materials as a way of consolidating the language points they had already taught their children, whereas for the validation teachers, these materials were often used to introduce a teaching session. This suggests that a similar point to that made about reading work also applies in the case of writing work. The effective teachers generally tried to ensure their teaching of language features was contextualised for their children and that the children understood the purpose of this teaching. Their chief means of achieving such contextualisation was to focus teaching on a shared text. Language features were taught, and explained to the children, as a means of managing this shared text rather than as a set of rules or definitions to be learnt for their own sakes.

- The effective teachers of literacy, because of their concern to contextualise their teaching of language features within shared text experiences, made explicit connections for their pupils between the text, sentence and word levels of language study.

- The lessons of the effective teachers were all conducted at a brisk pace. They regularly refocused children's attention on the task at hand and used clear time frames to keep children on task. They also tended to conclude their lessons by reviewing, with the whole class, what the children had done during the lesson. Lessons which ended with the teacher simply saying, 'We'll finish this tomorrow', were much more common among the validation teachers.

- The effective teachers used modelling extensively. They regularly demonstrated reading and writing to their classes in a variety of ways, often accompanying these demonstrations by verbal explanations of what they were doing. In this way they were able to make available to the children their thinking as they engaged in literacy.

- Some effective teachers differentiated the work they asked pupils to do by allotting different tasks on the basis of ability. These teachers also used another approach by varying the support given to particular groups of children when they were engaged on tasks the whole class would do at some point. By this means they were able to keep their classes working more closely together through a programme of work.

- The classrooms of the effective teachers were distinguished by the heavy emphasis on literacy in the environments which had been created. There were many examples of literacy displayed in these classrooms, these examples were regularly brought to the children's attentions and the children were encouraged to use them to support their own literacy.

- The effective teachers had very clear assessment procedures, usually involving a great deal of focused observation and systematic record-keeping. This contributed markedly to their abilities to select appropriate literacy content for their children's needs.

Analysis

The report from which this extract is taken has been very influential in the field of literacy education. The researchers used questionnaires, interviews and observations to study a group of 228 primary teachers who were identified as being effective teachers of literacy, and compared them with what they called a 'validation sample' of teachers who did not have literacy teaching as their specialism. They developed some very interesting conclusions that I want you to consider with your colleagues.

The belief systems of the effective teachers include an emphasis on purpose and meaning in their teaching. In other words, these teachers wanted their children to conceive of literacy as part of their world and not simply a school-based skills system. Interestingly, the effective teachers embedded more technical aspects of literacy knowledge within real contexts, often around real texts. I'm reminded here of Freebody's 'four roles' and the importance of teaching them together as a coherent whole in meaningful and purposeful ways. Of course, the emphasis is still on the printed word, but none the less the contextualisation of this form of literacy in real-world situations would inevitably involve embracing the literacy practices of children from other cultures.

Personal response

- Have you understood the significance of the arguments, issues and debates of this chapter?
- Write a short discussion paper of the main arguments found in this chapter. In your conclusion state your opinion and the significance this will have in your own teaching. Discuss this with colleagues.

Practical implications and activities

Explore the National Literacy Strategy *Framework for teaching* (DfEE, 1998). Begin to consider the possibilities and constraints of working with this document. Examine the text-based nature of the termly objectives to perceive the advantages of using well-written examples of children's literature. In addition, consider how other texts, like televisual, film or computer texts could be utilised to make literacy in school more like home.

Sit with a colleague and explore these possibilities.

In the next chapter you will have the opportunity to examine how beliefs about teaching a literacy will impact upon the classroom environment.

Writing activity

Commit yourself, with others, to begin a personal journal that documents the experiences you have while learning to be a teacher. You may wish to use digital means of doing this, or you may want to write it in a more conventional sense with pen and paper. By writing this journal you will be able to make more meaning out of what you are doing on your course and to experience the function and advantages of writing.

Further reading

Bearne, E (2003) 'Playing with possibilities: Children's multidimensional texts', in Bearne, E, Dombey, H and Grainger, T (eds) *Classroom interactions in literacy.* Maidenhead: Open University Press

Gee, J P (2004) *Situated language and learning: A critique of traditional schooling.* London: Routledge

Lankshear, C and Knobel, M (2003) *New literacies: Changing knowledge and classroom learning.* Buckingham: Open University Press

Marsh, J and Millard, E (2000) Introduction, in *Literacy and popular culture.* London: Paul Chapman

2 Preparing for literacy teaching and learning

By the end of this chapter you will have considered:

- **why** the environment teachers create in their classrooms is so important to how children learn;
- **what** a learning environment can reveal about the educational theories followed by the school;
- **how** you can plan for effective literacy learning in your class.

Professional Standards for QTS
3.1.3, 3.3.8

Children's literature read:
Lauren Child (2004), *I am absolutely too small for school*, Orchard Books.

Introduction

Every primary classroom you will walk into encapsulates the educational values held by the classroom teacher, school and the culture in which the institution belongs (Goodwin, 1999). When children come into the classroom, they too will 'read' and assess the classroom as a place in which they must live for up to six hours a day. They will look for ways that the environment may appeal to them and they will scrutinise the classroom for indications that they are welcome there. The previous chapter raised the issue of culture and the multicultural nature of literacy in society. All the chapters in this book are linked to this central concept, and the ways in which you as a teacher will organise and manage the environment for learning will also be intrinsically related. Your understanding of how children learn and your educational goals will influence the way you create your learning environment. For the teaching of English, the classroom will be determined by your conceptualisation of literacy and your understanding of how children learn to read, write, speak and listen. Equipped with an informed opinion on the fundamental principles of teaching and learning, you will begin the process of establishing the right environment for learning.

In addition to creating the physical environment for your classroom you will also need to establish how to utilise the spaces given to maximise the forms of learning that you will be passionately concerned to implement. The second half of this chapter concentrates on this issue.

Since the introduction of the National Literacy Strategy (DfEE, 1998) many teachers have been over-concerned to ensure coverage of all the objectives that are given in the framework document (OFSTED, 2005). Arguably, this has been at the expense of more coherent, holistic and meaningful experiences by a form of planning that gives children the time and opportunity to engage with the curriculum. Moreover, while the focus for teachers has been on coverage of the learning objectives found in the National Literacy Strategy's *Framework for teaching*, teachers have been less able to popularise the curriculum for the multiple literacy perspectives that children bring in to their classrooms (Jones, 2003). This requires a more improvisational, creative approach where teachers construct plans that are effective and challenging for the specific children in their class. There is research (Mroz et al, 2000) to suggest that the National Literacy Strategy's methods – shared reading/writing, guided reading/writing, plenary – although being very useful in certain situations, provide 'teaching technologies' that are not always appropriate for all children in all environments. The rigid and arguably static methods involved, modelled by many of the training videos that were sent out to schools by the Strategy managers, has led to teachers relinquishing their more professional improvisational teaching approaches that were more effective for the children in their class.

This chapter will ask you to explore and access the current 'units of work' model that has become popular in schools and that tries to provide more opportunity for teachers to tailor their planning for more extended and more meaningful learning episodes.

The physical environment

Places and spaces for learning

Before you read the extract, read:
- Chapter 1 in Geekie et al (1999) *Understanding literacy development*;
- 'Providing books; promoting learning', in Barrs and Browne (1991) *The reading book*.

Extract: Goouch, K (2005) 'Places and spaces for literacy', in Lambirth, A (ed) *Planning creative literacy lessons*. London: David Fulton.

Influences from research on pedagogy
A literate environment for children of all ages requires knowledge and understanding of the ways in which children develop and learn. Of course all children do not learn in the same way. Nevertheless there are key environmental elements that require careful thought and planning. For example, the choice between arranging desks in serried rows facing the front of a classroom or in groups where children face each other represents an understanding of how children most effectively think and learn. It would be naïve to believe that schools or classrooms or arrangements of learning spaces are in any sense neutral or devoid of cultural or philosophical influences. How desks are arranged, or whether or not to have desks at all, or how many desks to have, are all decisions that are influenced by cultural and professional cross-disciplinary decisions. Sociologists may argue that:

> What something is, what it does, one's evaluation of it – all this is not naturally preordained. It is socially constructed. This is the case even when we talk about the

institutions that organize a good deal of our lives. Take schools, for example …
(Apple, 2004:180)

Combined with such views, developmental psychologists argue that knowledge itself is socially constructed and that children actively, and in the company of others, construct their knowledge of the world which is 'shaped by their dialogues with the people around them' (Mercer, 2004:11). The work of Vygotsky (1978) and, later, Bruner (1986) provide support for the idea that knowledge is constructed by children 'rather than acquired by a process of accretion' (David et al., 2002) and that learners map together new knowledge with existing knowledge to make sense of their worlds. Both also emphasise the effect that other learners and supporting adults have in helping children to learn and depict learning as being most effective as a social act rather than a lone investigation. This model of learning indicates the necessity of designing and managing learning contexts with social groups in mind rather than individual recipients of fragments of knowledge. It also requires opportunities for active learning, which again has enormous implications for space and organisation which reflect this need.

As well as the social nature of learning, much research currently reflects the significance of culture in learning. Before school age, young children are inducted into literacy practices that have cultural significance in the home. It is within the social contexts of homes that young children's literacy development emerges and grows and Kress (1997) discusses the ways in which 'as children are drawn into culture, "what is to hand", becomes more and more that which the culture values and therefore makes readily available' (Kress 1997:13). Consequently, in cultures and communities where print has great significance, then children soon become encultured into sign making acts. In homes where families 'live with the litter of literacy' (Harste et al 1984:140) then children quickly become accustomed to using this 'cultural tool kit' (Kress 1997: 15) for purposes of expression. In families, the affective nature of literacy experiences and their everyday contextual occurrence engage children naturally in the use of appropriate materials and space for the activity. So, before school, for many children, literacy acts are often emotionally positive experiences, supported by appropriate resources, scaffolded by parents, carers or siblings, part of a social and cultural experience and therefore both engaging and self perpetuating. At home then, 'literacy and literate outcomes (are) processes to be experienced, to be placed in relation to other literacy events and practices rather than seen as unchanging objects of study or unquestioning reverence' (Bearne, 1995:4).

Recreating such a context within a classroom community may not be realistic. However, constructing and contriving opportunities for children to engage in reasonably authentic literacy practices, in the company of others and guided and supported by educators, is a real possibility. This requires a creative and committed view of the potential learning spaces provided in schools, combined with a clear view of the theories and principles that underpin such planning. The choices seem to be between a rather arid and narrow construction of the purposes of education and schooling, ie to confer the knowledge we (as educators) own to the next generation *or* rather more expansive notions of teaching and learning, relating to processes rather than performance and with a broader view of the nature of knowledge and the function of schools in society.

Great emphasis is currently placed upon the work of neuroscientists which has come to the attention of the popular press as well as professionals in the field of education. The work of, for example, Susan Greenfield has been particularly influential in debates about when and how the brain develops and critical periods of learning and, specifically, the effect of environments on brain development:

> If you put a rat in an enriched environment where there's things to play with, then even in adult rats you can see there is far more branching of the brain cells than in a control group. That's because even in adults, the more you stimulate the brain, the more it develops the potential for making connections … It's worth pointing out that an under-stimulating environment for children, given what we know about the human brain, would be ethically questionable. (Greenfield, 2002:21)

Sadly, however, this argument has been used to promote 'hot housing' of very young children. A more measured response has been to understand the research in terms of explaining the difference between 'normal' environments and deprived environments, rather than implying that 'special enriching experiences … beyond those that they experience in everyday life' are necessary for brain development (Blakemore 2002:29). Blakemore's interpretation is that 'there is a threshold of environmental richness below which a deprived environment could harm a (baby's) brain' (Blakemore 2002:29). The key evidence from neuroscience that is particularly useful to educators in planning appropriate environments for learning seems to be that:

- the cells that constitute the brain will proliferate at the staggering rate of 250,000 per minute
- young brains are exceptionally 'plastic' so they are shaped by experience
- stimulation for the brain is provided by conversations, experiences and encounters, irrespective of material wherewithal.
(adapted from Greenfield 2000, David et al 2002)

There is much to learn from the messages and implications from the combined disciplines of sociology, developmental psychology and neuroscience in relation to environments for literacy learning. Evidence across the research now appears to suggest that knowledge is socially constructed; culturally significant literacy practices engage children; effective learning practices are social in nature; and that a rich environment, encounters, interactions and experience have positive effects on developing brains.

Analysis

In this extract Goouch wants her readers to make links between the literacy of school and literacies of home through the creation of a learning environment. Consider the connections between what is being said here and in the previous chapter. Remember the important points made by O'Neil (1970) and his concept of 'proper literacy' – being able to draw on one's knowledge and experience and utilising it in new contexts. Goouch suggests that teachers need to construct environments in school that conceptualise and utilise literacy in similar ways to how literacies are seen and used in homes and in the wider context of society – in meaningful ways. The emphasis is placed on authenticity. Literacy is an organic entity that exists everywhere and is used in different ways in different social settings. 'Literacy' is not really a form of lesson at school; it fundamentally consists of all our communicative and cognitive repertoires. If one believes this to be true, then the classroom should reflect literacy and its uses outside of school. *The best theoretical accounts of learning and instruction are those which can be validated by reference to what real people do in natural contexts* (Geekie et al, 1999, p10). This seems to be the crux of Goouch's message concerning the construction of environments for literacy learning. The classroom needs to 'reference' the real world of literacy and multiple literacy events so children can make connections with what they know already and bring this to any new contexts and experiences that the teacher may seek to introduce.

As I said at the beginning of this chapter, the environment you construct in your classroom will be influenced by your educational goals. Wells (1981, p250) takes the view that: *although members of all cultures learn a mother tongue and use it effectively for the purposes of social and practical interaction, it is not the case that, in all cultures, the power inherent in language for symbolic representation is fully exploited in cognitive activity.* Wells' contention is that although it is important to respect and to utilise the knowledge and the experience of all the children's language repertoires, there are still things to be learned in order to maximise or 'amplify' (Bruner, 1972) these cultural resources. The environment should reflect this perspective. The space needs to be arranged to accommodate a dialogue between the children themselves and between the teacher and the children.

Teaching is not executed by *transferring knowledge from mind to mind, but through collaborative sessions in which children participate in acts of shared thinking with someone more competent than themselves* (Geekie et al, 1999, p10). Collaboration will be a crucial aspect that influences the design of the classroom environment, with the means to ensure that the more experienced can help those with less experience, which of course will include the more experienced teacher.

The classroom will also need to promote reading and writing and speaking and listening (Barrs and Browne, 1991; Goodwin, 1999; Grainger and Tod, 2000). A range of texts that both reflect the interests of the children and challenge them will need to be displayed prominently. Areas and equipment that promote imaginative 'world-making' should also be available to promote playful experiences that reflect the experiences of reading and writing. Most importantly of course, the physical environment created around the informed principles of the teacher will be enhanced by their enthusiasm, energy and interest and from whose passion the environment can only really take shape.

Personal response

- Talk to a teacher you have been working with about how her/his classroom is organised. Discuss the extent that the way the classroom is organised reflects the teacher's own educational values.
- Think about a classroom you have worked in. Did it illustrate your own beliefs about the teaching and learning of literacy?

Practical implications and activities

With a colleague, sit down and design your ideal literacy classroom for a particular year group that draws on the principles that you are developing. What kind of resources would there be? How would the tables be arranged? Why? Justify the choices you make with reference to learning theory and the curriculum.

Planning issues

Planning creative literacy lessons

Before you read the next extract, find the planning guidance from the National Primary Strategy for Literacy: **www.standards.dfes.gov.uk/primary/literacy/**
And read:

- Grainger, T (2005) 'Traditional tales and storytelling', in Lambirth (2005) *Planning creative literacy lessons.*

Extract: Lambirth, A (2005) 'Introduction: Planning creative literacy lessons', in Lambirth, A (ed) *Planning creative literacy lessons.* **London: David Fulton.**

Teachers as professionals and people

Since the advent of the National Curriculum (DES, 1989) and, more significantly, the introduction of the National Literacy Strategy (DfEE, 1998), the activity of Primary English teachers in their classrooms has greatly changed. There have been many debates amongst educationalists and politicians on how successful the recent National Strategies have been. What actually constitutes success is often the sticking point within these debates – is it the raising of standards as evidenced by government created tests? Or is it the less measurable effects on children's attitudes to reading and writing, or an improvement in creative approaches to pedagogy by teachers? Amongst the more indisputable negative results for teachers have been the sharp increases in workload, greater surveillance by line managers, head teachers and inspectors and a significant reduction in teacher autonomy. In addition, teachers' 'capacity to shape and popularise curricular practice' (Jones, 2003: 136) has been undermined by a shift from a focus on the *process*, to a *measurable product*, of teaching and learning. *Much of the emphasis in the NLS training materials has been on subject knowledge and content in the curriculum rather than pedagogy, so that teaching styles have only been superficially addressed* (Mroz, Smith & Hardman, 2000:387).

Arguably the English curriculum, as conceptualised in the National Literacy Strategy Framework for teaching (DfEE, 1998), is to be delivered, regardless of cultural specificity, to 'pupils' as an autonomous package called 'literacy' in an environment of teacher and pupil compliance. The implementation of the Strategy has attempted to dispense with the professional questions about the process of teaching and learning that were alive between teachers in earlier decades, replaced by a standard prescriptive programme. Yet, teachers and educationalists have always known that establishing prescribed 'indisputable' answers to teaching questions will only bring forth more questions.

Within an atmosphere, of almost at times, educationally servile conditions, there is a danger, as a teacher, to feel that there is a need to remove one's personal and individually determined contribution. The role of the teacher might well be construed as just a deliverer of learning, mediated by a strategy document. The personal significance of the individual teacher's background, experience, culture and character might even appear redundant, inappropriate and unwanted. Consequently, there are real dangers that classrooms become sterile, devoid of human character, warmth and the individual personality of the teaching professional. The urgency for pace and the dogged determination to deliver learning objectives, stressed in the Strategy documents (DfEE, 1998), mould the nature of literacy lessons away from the encouragement of a sense of community and a sharing of culture and interest, formed by a sustained dialogue between teachers and children.

There is a belief that the place of a teacher's individual character is key in constructing an atmosphere of fruitful teaching and learning. This belief is based on a view that effective teaching must have the 'x factor' of artistic input that can only be supplied by galvanising the creative capacities of individual teachers. The main aim of this book, therefore, is to help rekindle the 'x factor' and to encourage teachers to be artists in their own classrooms (Grainger, Goouch & Lambirth, 2005).

Literacy teaching for children in the here and now

The generation of creative activities for the teaching of English forms part of the *process* of teaching and learning. Creativity, therefore, has fallen foul to the ferocious determination by government agencies to ensure that schools effectively produce measurable learning *product* by the use of unquestionable methods. The suppression of creative-process-models of teaching in schools reflects the vision of contemporary government:

> The role of government in this world of change is to represent a national interest, to create a competitive base of physical infrastructure and human skills. The challenge before our party … is not to slow down and so get off the world, but to educate and retrain for the next technologies, to prepare our country for new global competition, and to make our country a competitive base from which to produce the goods and services people want to buy.
> (Blair, 1995:20)

The drive to 'prepare' Britain for the world market has clearly impacted upon educational policy of successive governments over the last fifteen years or so. The overall thrust has been to give children and young people the skills they need for the market place – to be able to compete in changing technological conditions and environments – offering the capacity for inter-changeable skills and increased 'labour power'. This is the philosophy of a 'developmental state' (Lee, 2001), determined to prepare for 'tomorrow'.

Primary schools are of course concerned to prepare children for what will come, but ignoring what is now may have an adverse effect upon the future. A method of schooling that puts too much emphasis on what society wants children to become conceptualises children, not as 'human beings', existing in the here and now but more, as 'human becomings' (Lee, 2001). The only way to achieve full human being status is by adopting the roles prepared for them by the socialisation processes of society. For New Labour this appears to be a young person's adaptability as workers within the global market and undermines the possibility of individual creative capacities and critical approaches to learning: *Adulthood and full humanity is the achievement of independence, confidence and certainty through the acquisition of knowledge of one's place in society* (Lee, 2001: 39).

Yet we know that the genuine process of education involves recognition of children as social human beings (Geekie, Cambourne & Fitzsimmons, 1999), where learning depends upon the negotiation of meanings and where those who lead the learning also follow (Wood, 1992). Children will not respond well as learners if they are regarded simply as recipients of supplementation.

Analysis

If you have had the opportunity to visit the National Primary Strategy's website, you will have seen how the exemplification materials provided present a plan for teaching that has a duration of around two weeks and is based upon particular written genres. As I am encouraging you to do with this book, you need to approach this material critically, utilising what you feel would be usefully applied to the children for whom you have responsibility. In the extract provided here, I write about planning that highlights the need for teachers to retain their own professionalism and creativity and not feel bound to implement all aspects of the exemplification materials provided by governments. It may feel safer to do so, but in my experience, if the materials fail to be effective with your own class, life begins to become much harder anyway. I want to draw your attention to the units of work's more positive aspects in relation to the extract that you have just read.

Working in units of work provides the opportunity to enjoy and learn about a wide range of written texts over a sustained period of time. Research (Frater, 2000; Barrs and Cork, 2001) has highlighted the importance of children being exposed to different forms of writing in order to enhance their own writing and to learn from models of effective and enjoyable literature. Rigidly adhering to two-week blocks does not provide enough flexibility, so the duration needs to be variable. It does, however, allow children time to become immersed in the texts, exploring their meanings and examining why they are so successful in a variety of creative and collaborative ways. Of course, the texts that the National Literacy Strategy suggest are all from the printed word. But creative teachers will be able to find means to incorporate televisual and digital texts (Marsh and Millard, 2000; Marsh, 2005), drawing on the experiences and practices of literacy that the children bring to the classroom.

The progression from reading to writing within a unit of work provides powerful opportunities for children to experiment with writing in these forms (Barrs and Cork, 2001). Indeed, *reading and writing are two halves of the same process: that of mastering language* (Barrs and Cork, 2001, p42) and therefore this form of planning sequence seems essential. However, the units can also integrate reading, writing, speaking and listening, because many of the activities throughout the plan will inevitably involve all three strands. The collaborative work involved in drama activities, storytelling and general discussion will also demand the need to talk and write for various purposes.

The emphasis on texts provides opportunities to teach within real contexts and enables teachers to combine the 'four roles of literacy', as Freebody (1992) describes them. Moreover, if teachers feel empowered to avoid the 'teaching technologies' that do not suit their class and begin to improvise on the genuine needs of the children, they will be able to exert their full creative capacities for the teaching of literacy.

Personal response

- To what extent do you feel free to implement the practice you know to be right from extensive reading within educational literature?
- Set up a discussion with a group of your colleagues. If you have access to electronic communication systems, start a discussion with the whole of your group.
- If you feel restricted in how you can teach your children, where does this come from and why?

Practical implications and activities

Work with another colleague on producing your own set of plans based on the units of work model. Draw on other readings and advice to assist you. How would you ensure that your plans include activities that will stimulate and motivate your class? Share your plans with others in your group.

Find other examples of explicit planning advice from published materials e.g. Letts, LCP, Scholastic. These should be whole plans that have been devised to assist teachers in their planning on a termly, weekly and daily basis. Examine them critically using your own framework, based upon your reading of good practice.

In the next chapter you will look at issues concerning the teaching of reading.

Writing activity

Consider the form of creative/fictional writing you know the best. Attempt a piece of writing in this form on a subject of your choice. Try and craft your work by drafting and redrafting the writing. Share it with a colleague and start making a collection of the writing you are doing.

Further reading

Barrs, M and Cork V (2001) *The reader in the writer: The links between the study of literature and writing development at Key Stage 2.* London: Centre for Literacy in Primary Education

Lambirth, A (ed) (2005) *Planning creative literacy lessons.* London: David Fulton

3 Teaching reading

By the end of this chapter you will have considered:

- **why** reading has become such an area of contention;
- **what** the basics of the teaching of reading are and some of the main issues involved in this area of literacy teaching;
- **how** you should approach the teaching of phonics.

Professional Standards for QTS
3.3.2b, 3.3.7, 3.3.8

Children's literature read:
Jack Prelutsky and Lane Smith (2001), *Dr Seuss: Hooray for Diffendoofer Day!*, Collins.

Introduction

In this chapter you will consider some important issues about the teaching and learning of reading. This area of literacy teaching has a raft of issues that you will need to examine in order to fully understand how children learn to read. I have chosen to concentrate on what might be called the 'basics' of reading. The concept of the basics of reading has multiple interpretations and this is what I want you and your colleagues to explore. You will quickly begin to discern my own beliefs about reading from my own choice of theoretical extracts and from what I say. So you should remain critical.

Over many years there has been much debate on how children learn to read and, consequently, how they should be taught. The debate has become polarised over time and this has oversimplified the positions. For example, the media often set up artificial warring factions between groups constructed as the 'phonics brigade' and the 'real books army'. The former group demands the prioritisation of the teaching of phonics skills and the latter group insists that children learn to read by reading and hearing 'real' books (authored books rather than reading schemes written to 'teach' reading) read to them. In reality both perspectives offer a more complex position. There is no doubt that people would like learning to read to be very simple, but sadly this is not the case. It is a highly complex process, as mind-boggling as rocket science to understand, but arguably of greater importance to human development at all levels. However, research into reading over the last 30 years has increased our knowledge of the process and we do know that: *Reading is much more than the decoding of black marks upon the page: it is a quest for meaning and one which requires the reader to be an active participant* (Cox, 1989).

The notion of 'activity as central to understanding the principles of reading' is where this chapter will begin. I want you to explore the *experience* of reading. It could be argued that novice readers will need to know and fully appreciate the attractions of the journey through a book before they will choose to spend their valuable time indulging in reading. Therefore, this might be described as the basics of reading – understanding its purposefulness, meaningfulness and its general affordance. The first extract attempts to describe part of this experience.

The next piece comes from an excellent book on reading by Professor Kathy Hall. It describes one of a range of perspectives that have been very influential and controversial in teaching. It looks at reading as a quest for meaning that mirrors the quotation from Cox that was given above.

The final two extracts are there to examine the debate over the teaching of phonics. People are passionate about this issue and it has become highly politically charged. I feel it is important that you have the opportunity to discuss the issues and feel comfortable about where you stand when you begin to take responsibility for the reading development of children in your class. It will be a political area of reading teaching that you will encounter time and time again.

The basics

What happens when we read stories?
Before you read the extract, read:
- Barrs and Browne (1991) 'Understanding reading', in *The reading book*;
- Stierer, B (2002) 'Simply doing their job? The politics of reading standards and "real books"', in Solar et al. *Contextualising difficulties in literacy development: Exploring politics, culture, ethnicity and ethics.*

Extract: Benton, M and Fox, G (1985) 'What happens when we read stories?', in *Teaching literature nine to fourteen*, pp4–6. Oxford: Oxford University Press.

a) Where does the secondary world exist?
When we write or read we enter, as Tolkien suggests, an imaginative limbo, an in-between state of mind which draws upon both the psychic make-up of an individual and the actual world that is everyone's possession. This 'third area' as D. W. Winnicott has called it, is best thought of as a sort of mental playground in which makers and readers of stories can operate in relative freedom and security. The time and place of the primary world fade and are replaced by the time and place that the story decrees. We become 'lost' in a book or, more precisely, in an imaginative game that entails writer or reader constructing an alternative world to replace the one that the book has temporarily obliterated. The world we make is not literal: it has presence and power to engage and move us but no substance with which to threaten. Indeed, for the adult reader, the 'security' of a novel may well be reflected by a relished routine: the comfortable chair, the familiar lamp, a drink to sip. Children who read regularly talk of specific areas of their homes where they prefer to read: their beds, the bath or, oblivious to domestic tension, the lavatory, are places where young readers report that they lose themselves in their books. The trick is to shut out one world to enter another.

It seems my ears switch off, and my mum's just standing there yelling her head off, and I just sit there reading.

The reader's physical contentment releases, and reinforces, a frame of mind:

> I read mostly on the side by my bed, on the floor where it is nice and quiet and if my sister comes up I can duck my head down;

and even,

> I like reading standing on my head on the sofa because I like to practise upside down.

Whatever physical contortions we get up to we can play the game in our own imaginative style, take our pleasure from it in the way we want and stop playing when we choose. Yet, this game, like any other, has rules and conventions which must be observed. Even infants (perhaps they most of all) know this.

Children learn early that words are powerful makers of stories. Whatever their individual difficulties in coming to terms with print, all children seem responsive to oral story-telling. The two conventions that sustain their responses are the willingness to believe in an acknowledged illusion and the need to know the end. The insubstantial fabric of story is created and supported by these twin pressures. Belief in the illusion gives a sense of place to the world of story and grows out of the child's easy exploration of the relationship between the actual and the fantasized in his play. The sense of an ending gives it a temporal dimension and reflects the need to know what happens next, a need which quickly develops into a sense of structure of beginnings, middles and endings and comprises a fundamental part of the child's imaginative investment in fiction.

Words are toys, playthings with which to make up a game in the head. The ease with which a two or three year old inhabits both the world that is and the world that might be and shifts effortlessly between the two, is a facility that dims with age, however hard we fight to retain our sense of play. Where teachers and parents can help is in nourishing and preserving the childlike sense of story as a play activity.

As a child gets older, whatever his ability as a reader, one principle remains constant: reading is idiosyncratic. How a child reads reflects his whole person so that to read at all inevitably involves the stored experiences of the reader and his characteristic ways of being and acting. In the act of creating, what the reader brings to a story is as important as what the text offers in the sense that we fit the reading of a new story into the blend of our literary and life experiences to date, drawing upon our knowledge of other fictions as well as upon analogies in the primary world, in order to make our own, unique meaning.

The answer, then, to our first question, 'Where does the secondary world exist?' is that it lies in an area of play activity between the reader's inner reality and the outer reality of the words on the page. The world of the book draws its idiosyncratic nature from the former and is shaped by the latter. Different readers' responses to a story thus have enough in common to be shared while remaining highly individual. The literature classroom becomes a place where pupils may gain from others' responses while preserving their sense of uniqueness as readers.

b) What is the secondary world made of?

If the reading experience is an amalgam of individual associations and memories mingling with more precisely traceable reactions provoked by the text, how does the infinite variety of this world manifest itself? The commonest answer, but not the only one, is by way of mental imagery – pictures which form in the reader's head. Writers and readers frequently testify to their visual sense of the world they imagine. Less frequently they refer to auditory images and only relatively rarely to those drawn from the other senses. If we accept that mental imagery is the prime coinage of the brain during the creative activity of writers and readers, several caveats must be entered immediately. First, that the use made of images varies greatly from one person to the next. Secondly, that an important aspect of this variability is in the degree of mental control that any individual exercises. The images that the mind constructs to fill the 'third area' may arrive unbidden like those of night-dreams or, like those of day-dreams, be indulged or banished at will. Writers and readers need both bidden and unbidden images to make their secondary worlds. The writer shapes his images, via the use of words, into a text; the reader shapes the text, via the use of images, into a meaning. The role of images, thus delimited, leads us to the third point: images are a means to an end, not the end itself. It is the *manner* in which the secondary world is made by each reader that endows it with personally significant meaning. Indeed, there are some who appear to experience little picturing during reading, claiming to have merely the sense of being *in the presence* of a world. Also, most habitual readers have had the sensation of thinking in pure meanings when, in periods of profound engrossment in a story, the mind may by-pass imaging as a means to comprehending.

Analysis

The phrase 'response to literature' is rather under-used in the official curriculum documents on literacy teaching. The word 'comprehension' is used far more often, for example as part of the 'text level' objectives in the National Literacy Strategy *Framework for teaching* (DfEE, 1998). Yet, appreciating our own internal responses and experiences to stories would seem to me to be an important motivating factor in becoming a committed reader. It is one thing to be *able* to read and another to *want* to do it, but there is an intrinsic connection between the two. Surely, it is part of a teacher's responsibility to generate the desire to read in young children, for as a consequence children will practise more often and become more technically competent too. So, getting 'back to basics' in the teaching of reading must include getting children 'hooked' on books and stories because of the rich rewards gathered from the experience of being a reader.

Understanding the reading experience is not easy. Benton (1978, p16) contends that it is:

> the Loch Ness Monster of literary studies. When we set out to capture it we can not even be sure that it is there at all and, if we assume it is, we have to admit that the most sensitive probing with the most sensitive instruments has so far succeeded in only producing pictures of dubious authenticity.

The process is private and purely cognitive, which will defy translation into speech. Wolfgang Iser (1976, p35) writes that the *effect is in the nature of experience and not an exercise in explanation.* Yet, accomplished readers do testify to an active and dynamic interaction with the text – an extension to symbolic play (Sarland, 1982) – which requires the reader to draw on their own experiences of life and other stories to create their own unique meaning. This will include images and sounds in one's head. Sustained reading will eventually result in the mental episodic disappearance of the primary world in favour of the secondary world generated by the unique combination of the imaginations of author and reader. This is an extraordinary phenomenon, and I believe that there are many people, both adults and children, who are unaware of this almost hallucinogenic cognitive experience. This happening is the result of a reader's interaction with words. Bates (1979) describes the word as being like an iceberg. The tip represents the public aspect of its meaning; below is the submerged base of private meaning that the reader constructs in relation to his or her understanding of the world. This might well be considered one of the basics of reading – understanding its personal pleasures and life-enhancing cognitive journeys.

As teachers you will need to create ways for children to begin to experience real reading and the pleasures of which it forms part. You will need to consider how this can happen. Examine the similarities between the reading experience and play, the emphasis on pleasure and the imagination and the need for powerful, well-written stories that draw children into their world. Think about how exploring personal meanings could emphasise the individual nature of the experience. Unlike the situation with comprehension exercises, an exploration of personal response can yield no 'wrong' answers, simply because there are no 'right' ones, no absolutes. Discussion of literature should be an unthreatening activity, where readers can feel free to voice their own individual perspectives. You should also think about exploring secondary worlds through the use of drama and role-play. This way the worlds are brought out of the book and into the classroom within which children can play.

Personal response

- With a partner, discuss what happens to you when you read a novel. Find out how this compares with others. Do you recognise the concept of a secondary world?
- 'Snowball' your conversation by joining with another pair and then another to make a six.
- Discuss a piece of fiction that engulfed you in another world.
- Is there anyone in your group who does not know the reading experience? How do they become lost in fiction – through film, theatre, computer games? Discuss the similarities of experience between these modes of communication. If you do agree on similarities, is reading a book 'better' than 'reading' a film? Who says so and why?

Practical implications and activities

Meet with some colleagues and decide how you could emphasise the reading experience in your classroom. Think in terms of teaching methods, resources and environment.

> Read from a book to some children in your class. Engage the children in activities that will raise the individual meaning-making that takes place when you read – try some drama, small-group discussion or role-play.

Quest for meaning

Reading as a problem-solving activity

Before you read the next extract, read:

- Meek (1991) 'Why are stories special?', in *On being literate*;
- Hall (2003) 'A cognitive-psychological perspective', in *Listening to Stephen read*.

Extract: Hall, K (2003) 'Reading as a problem solving activity', in *Listening to Stephen read: Multiple perspectives on literacy*, pp37–41. Buckingham: Open University Press.

Whence the psycho-linguistic perspective?

The linguist Noam Chomsky (1965) revolutionized the study of language when he demonstrated that comprehending language was not a matter of linking up the various meanings of adjacent words. This kind of linear processing was the basis of the behaviourist psychologists' accounts of language comprehension that had prevailed for some fifty years before. Children did not simply imitate the language they heard, Chomsky suggested. Language was far too complex to be acquired in this way. He postulated a nativist view of language acquisition in suggesting that humans are innately predisposed to acquire the language of their environment. Children naturally acquire the language of the home by sheer exposure, he observed, and they become good users of oral language long before they start school. Moreover, they become proficient in oral language without direct instruction. In Chomsky's view, humans had to be equipped with some cognitive device for working out the complex rules of language – how else could you explain this remarkable achievement?

Many in the field of reading, especially psychologists, then began to wonder if Chomsky's observations about oral language could also be applied to written language. This was how a psycho-linguistic position on reading came about. While Chomsky had argued that children were innately equipped to learn language, psycho-linguists went on to demonstrate that children were active learners who worked out the rules of language for themselves. When a child says 'I eated my dinner', or 'I can see two sheeps' s/he is inferring that you put an event in the past by adding 'ed' to the verb and that you make a noun plural by adding 's'. So mistakes in their oral language give insights into the way children were inferring the rules. Could there be parallels in written language? Do children learn how to read and to write in much the same way as they acquired oral language? Could learning to read and to write be natural?

Reading as natural and as a constructive or problem-solving activity

These questions exercised several literacy researchers but perhaps few more so than Kenneth and Yetta Goodman and Frank Smith. Kenneth Goodman argued that the mistakes, or what he termed 'miscues', children make while reading are better viewed as information about the comprehending process the reader is going through than mistakes to be eliminated. They should be viewed, he argued, as indicators of how the reader was making sense of the text. He concluded that, because children were better able to read words in story contexts than in word lists, they were using context knowledge to support comprehension and word identification. It's important to note that reading, according to Goodman, depends not only on the text but also on what the reader brings to the text in the form of previous knowledge, not just of language, but knowledge of the world itself. He says:

> Reading is a constructive process: both the text and the meaning are constructed by the reader. That means that at any point in time there are two or more texts during reading: the published text and the reader's text. In the transactions, both the reader and the text are changed. The reader's knowledge and schemata are changed, and the text is changed as the reader constructs it to fit expectations and world knowledge. In this emerging consensus, what the reader brings to the text is as important as anything in the text. Comprehension always depends on the reader's knowledge, beliefs, schemata, and language ability.
> (Goodman 1992: 358)

Overall, emphasis is placed on the meaning that learners themselves want to communicate.

His close observation and analysis of actual reading behaviour led him to describe reading as 'a psycho-linguistic guessing game' (Goodman 1967). Here he laid out the elements of language that he thought readers used to construct meaning from texts. He suggested that readers draw on three cue systems simultaneously to make sense of text: graphophonic, syntactic, and semantic cues. He said:

> The readers of English I have studied utilize three cue systems simultaneously. The starting point is graphic in reading and we may call one cue system 'graphophonic'. The reader responds to graphic sequences and may utilize the correspondence between the graphic and phonological systems of his English dialect … The second cue system the readers uses is 'syntactic'. The reader using pattern markers such as function words and inflectional suffixes as cues recognizes and predicts and structures … The third cue system is 'semantic'. In order to derive meaning from language, the language user must be able to provide semantic input. This is not simply a question of meaning for words but the much larger question of the reader having sufficient experience and conceptual background to feed into the reading process so that he can make sense out of what he's reading …
> (Goodman 1973: 25–6)

By using all these cue systems readers could minimize uncertainty about unknown words and meanings. Since readers are viewed to be naturally motivated to make sense of texts, Goodman saw no reason to distinguish between a word-identification phase and a comprehension phase in reading nor to isolate any single cue system for separate training or development. He said 'We can study how each one (cue system) works in reading and writing, but they can't be isolated for instruction without creating non-language abstractions' (Goodman 1986: 38-9).

Similarly, Frank Smith's *Understanding Reading* (1971) argued that reading was not something that you are taught, but rather something you learned to do as a consequence of belonging to a literate society and he postulated that there were no special prerequisites to learning to read. He said 'The function of teachers is not so much to "teach" reading as to help children read' (1971: 3). For him, you learn to read by reading and you learn to write by writing. In line with Goodman's notion of reading as a psycho-linguistic guessing game, Smith suggested that reading was a matter of making informed predictions about a text based on what readers already knew about how language works (syntactic and semantic knowledge) and what they knew about the world (semantic knowledge). His idea was that the reader develops hunches or hypotheses about upcoming words in a text and then confirms what the word is by sampling only a few features of the visual display. He advanced the controversial idea that reading was only incidentally visual – he minimized the role that graphic information plays in reading, saying:

> The more difficulty a reader has with reading, the more he relies on the visual information; this statement applies to both the fluent reader and the beginner. In each case, the cause of the difficulty is inability to make full use of syntactic and semantic redundancy, of nonvisual sources of information. (Smith 1971: 221)

And two years later he reiterated the secondary importance of visual information in saying 'It is clear that the better reader barely looks at the individual words on the page' (Smith 1973: 190). By nonvisual sources he meant readers' prior knowledge of the context and of the way language works. He argued for the importance of these sources of information so readers could make good predictions and so they would not have to rely too heavily on visual information, thus losing sight of the meaning.

Even more controversially, Smith (1973: 105) claimed that 'readers do not use (and do not need to use) the alphabetic principle of decoding to sound in order to learn to identify words'. To reiterate Smith's position: in coming to the text with expectations and a disposition to predict, readers sample just enough of it to confirm or reject their predictions. As will be demonstrated below, this take on reading and, in particular, the status Smith (and others) attributed to graphophonic knowledge have since been challenged and found to be inaccurate.

Basically psycho-linguists, like the Goodmans and Smith, view writing as paralleling oral language, differing only in mode. In 1980 Yetta Goodman claimed 'Language development is natural whether written or oral. It develops in a social setting because of the human need to communicate and interact with the significant others in the culture' (Goodman 1980: 3). Written language is seen as having the same functions as all other forms of language (listening, speaking) which include the need to inform, to communicate, to interact with others, to learn about the world and so on. In other words, language, whatever its mode, serves a purpose for the learner; young children learn to talk because it is useful and functional for them. So the argument goes that if written language is also seen as functional, then children will learn to produce (write) and understand it (read) in much the same way. And just as oral language is learned without direct teaching, so too written language could be learned without direct intervention. In this country several theorists advocated greater links across the various modes of language and they raised awareness of the power of language as a medium of learning (e.g. Barnes *et al.* 1972; Britton 1972; Barnes 1981; Corden 2000).

The Goodmans (1979) actually assumed that there was only one reading process, that is that all readers, whether beginner/inexperienced or fluent/experienced use the same process, although they differ in the control they have over the process. They assumed a non-stage reading process, in other words. In their view the major advantage experienced readers have over inexperienced ones is their better knowledge of language and of the world. As such, skilled readers, it was thought, relied less on orthographic information.

The teacher's role in this model involves two things: first, creating a climate in which children would be interested in using reading and writing – as Newman (1985) put it, offering 'invitations' to learn – and second, enabling children join the 'literacy club' as Smith (1992). In this view reading development is best fostered through exposure to text that is rich in natural language and through helping the reader attend to meanings and contexts. It is assumed that controlling the vocabulary of texts or attending to parts of words would not pay dividends; that in fact such an approach would limit opportunities for learning.

In this context Wade (1990) debated the inadequacies of the reading schemes of the time in this country, providing an instance from one in which reading in reverse order from line eighteen to line one, rather than from line one to eighteen, appeared to make as much (or as little!) sense. He argued that the short sentences, the simple vocabulary and repetition of sounds, words and ideas limited the reader's meaning-making and prediction potential. Similarly Margaret Meek (1988) criticized the disconnective text, the insubstantial characters and the lack of interest or suspense in the train of events in reading schemes, contrasting this with the richness of language and satisfying plots associated with children's literature.

Because reading is seen to develop 'from whole to part, from vague to precise, from gross to fine, from highly concrete and contextualized to more abstract' (Goodman 1986: 39) this perspective on the reading process is often thought of as a 'top-down' model of literacy development. Whole stories are seen as better than sentences and sentences are seen as better than words (Holdaway 1979). Dividing language into smaller and smaller parts or subskills jeopardizes clarity, meaning and simplicity, it is assumed. While the teaching of 'basic language skills' is not ruled out, it is recommended that they are developed within a wider language context which can make vital contributions to the efficiency and organization of the classroom for learning. Both Ann Browne and Teresa Grainger stressed this point about integration and sense of purpose in their deliberations about Stephen. In fact both scholars gave this the status of a principle of learning. They spoke about the importance of purpose, relevance and of intrinsic motivation. Ann asked: 'Does he understand what reading is for?' and Teresa's unease about the teacher's affirmations for word accuracy shows her contention that reading and learning are largely based on intrinsic motivation and personal relevance rather than on extrinsic rewards and the proddings of others.

Analysis

Hall's discussion and analysis of the work of psycholinguists should make you consider the practice you have already seen in schools. You will no doubt find many examples of this perspective applied in the teaching methods and the environments you have observed. Some key points to note are that these thinkers maintain that all language, whether spoken or written, is always used for authentic purposes. As a consequence, the practices that the psycholinguists prescribe involve reading and writing in real communicative situations. They would condemn decontextualised skills practice or language drills divorced from real-life, meaningful interactions with texts. Like Chomsky's views on spoken language acquisition, their belief is that children will learn the skills and practices they need to read through authentic, meaningful engagement with written language. This means not offering children graded and staged, step-by-step skills teaching, but instead they want teachers to offer the children 'whole' literacy experiences in real situations and this is why this school of thought is known as the 'whole-language' approach. Frank Smith (1978) identified two basic necessities for learning to read: a mass of interesting and engaging materials with which young readers can identify and enjoy, and an understanding adult who can guide the children. If the acquisition of the skills needed to understand written language comes from a natural quest for meaning, as in Chomsky's description of the acquisition of spoken language, then interaction with written text in authentic communicative situations will be a key aim for teachers.

However, the word 'natural' seems to suggest that learning to read can be as natural as learning to talk. But acquiring spoken language is biologically supported – it's a kind of instinct to learn to talk (Gee, 2004). Over thousands of years humans have developed a language instinct (Pinker, 1994) and this provides the biological capability to learn to talk. Reading is a relatively new process and therefore has not had the evolutionary time to become part of our inner make-up and capability. Oral communication has become an instinct; reading has not. However, this may not mean that learning to read needs only a clear instructional path, characterised by drills and skills. In my view, children need to be provided with an environment that makes learning to read important. A culture needs to be created (Gee, 2004) around books and stories and multiple meanings, where reading is seen as vital, exciting and 'natural'. Here the whole-language approach appears still to be a powerful model.

Again, I'm sure you will be making connections with the reading extracts of earlier chapters. Examples could include Goouch's argument for authentic environments and O'Neil's (1970) demand for 'proper literacy' and Freebody's (1992) contention in the Lankshear and Knobel (2002) reading that his four roles of literacy need to be taught together at all phases of education.

Personal response

- Consider your own reading development as a child. Did you learn to read because of the reading methods adopted by the teachers and adults around you, or did you learn in spite of them?
- Were you given access to books that would interest you or were they books that were thought of as necessary to 'teach' you to read?

Practical implications and activities

Sit with a child and listen to them read. Do a 'running record' or a miscue analysis while you listen (see Further reading at the end of this chapter). Then have a general discussion about reading with the child in order to establish the child's attitude to reading. Next, sit down with a colleague who has completed the same exercise and discuss the children's progress as readers.

Phonics

Politics and research

Before you read the next two extracts, read:

- Coles (2000) 'Erecting the strong consensus', in *Misreading reading.*

Extract: Davis, Jr, O L (2002) 'When will the phonics police come knocking?', in Solar, J, Wearmouth, J and Reid, G (eds) *Contextualising difficulties in literacy development: Exploring politics, culture, ethnicity and ethics*, pp83–86. London: RoutledgeFalmer.

Phonics is 'in'. This reality is no longer news. Indeed, advocates promote phonics as the 'one best system' in American education for the initial teaching of reading. They seek more than the replacement of the whole-word approach. Phonics also serves as the emblem of the increasingly aggressive crusade to rid schooling of the alleged blights of a polluted and rancid progressivism. This movement's anthem well might be 'The World Turned Upside Down'.

To be sure, teachers and educational leaders in the United States have weathered previous political storms over reading instruction. They have resisted the simplistic folly of either-or instructional proposals. As a matter of fact, they have continued their steady work amidst strident charges of failure from rival opposition forces.

These previous tempests mainly were rhetorical. The work of education continued to be practical. For example, advocates of phonics and whole-word approaches have competed for rhetorical dominance for more than a century. At various times, one or another approach became fashionable, even popular, at conference sessions, in journal accounts, and even in textbooks and teachers' lounges. By and large, teachers mainly ignored the swirling winds of advocacy or temporarily coopted the new slogan to describe their practice. They continued to teach individual children as they believed most appropriate and adopted as their own some elements of the 'new' procedures that made sense to them. No matter which advocacy group claimed victory, most teachers of reading continued to teach in the very best ways they knew. Their 'best' continually improved. A wealth of solid educational research across the entire century has informed their practice.

Even so, not all children have learned to read well. Many, certainly too many, have failed to learn to read. Even after mindful diagnosis and the use of carefully crafted, individually designed programmes some individuals read only haltingly or not at all. No teacher, no administrator – at least, none in my experience – remains unmoved by such results. They want their pupils to learn to read. They want to do more. Typically, they try some other procedure, invent or adapt another approach. The existence of nonreading children and adults constitutes a monumental frustration and loss to those individuals – as well as to their teachers.

The great majority of US teachers of reading are likely to continue to use both of the major contested approaches – and others – as they seek to help children with different talents and backgrounds to learn to read. To be sure, individual teachers prefer one or some approaches over others. Nevertheless, teachers follow the general pattern of generations of their predecessors. They use whatever procedures they know or can devise or have at hand to help their students learn to read. Significantly, most administrators have supported their teachers' intense and balanced efforts.

The current contest over reading continues to be rhetorical, of course, but it differs from earlier reading wars. It is more an intense political campaign of ideological zealots than it is a controversy. Several changed features dominate its landscape. Most importantly, the present controversy is *not* professional; it is *not* about influence. It is public, impressively political and bureaucratic, and about absolute ideological control.

Proponents of phonics-only instruction appear to have captured the attention and power of several key state governors and state boards of education. Consequently, they have dominated these states' new standards for reading instruction not only about specific goals. They are now working to mandate that phonics be the standard instructional procedure to teach reading throughout the state. Among their tactics is legislation that mandates phonics-only reading instruction in a state's public schools. Their influence over the bureaucratic links between state-mandated standards and professional teacher and administrator licensure already has produced a nightmarish vision of government intrusion into higher education. This horrid spectre erupts from serious proposals that all accredited educator preparation programmes in a state must employ common syllabi that feature phonics-only reading instruction. In the current situation, phonics proponents appear to be following a 'take no prisoners' position. Already real are early casualties: they are responsible, serious teachers.

Can the phonics police be far behind? When will they come knocking at schoolhouse doors? Will they handcuff errant teachers as pupils watch? Or will they apprehend the teacher or administrator at home in the darkness of the night?

This dismal vision of the near future appears at once to be outrageous and monumentally bizarre. On the other hand, it could happen and it could occur soon. Legislated phonic instruction must define legal and illegal instructional practice and establish punishments for violations of the law. Some agency (and it could be a new 'Corps of Phonics Police') must be the enforcers of the law. Violators – in this case, teachers and college professors, perhaps administrators, school systems, and universities – must be prosecuted. What might be the penalties for the use of an illegal procedure to teach reading? Public censure? Suspension or revocation of teaching licence? Dismissal? Fines? Imprisonment?

Less possibly imagined would be proposals to legislate practice in other professions. For example, a legislative requirement that defence attorneys employ a prescribed strategy without regard to the specifics of the alleged crime, its circumstances, and the defendant seems unthinkable. Similarly, legislation that would require surgery as the only treatment for all cancers, no matter the type of their cells or their spread or the patient's individual history, is ludicrous. For the teaching of reading, however, politicians appear eager to accept as appropriate the selection of just one procedure for all children in every situation.

In the present tortured uncertainty, phonics-only advocates usually influence politicians and bureaucrats behind public view. Therefore, most Americans, including most education professionals, remain 'out of the loop' until agencies announce freshly written administrative mandates. The legislative process, however, remains more open than are the labyrinths of bureaucratic operations. The political takeover of educational practice, even at this late hour, still can be frustrated. The chilling prospects of the phonics police can be avoided, but not without responsible action.

Obviously, the situation is grave, and easy answers are unavailable. On the other hand, American citizens and, especially, the nation's educational leaders and teachers must recognize the certain perils of inaction. Not just reading programmes and reading teachers are in peril. Emboldened by success in the phonics-only battles, the proponents surely will target additional school subjects. Little imagination is required to wonder what legislation may follow for the teaching of other school subjects; surely, biology, history, and literature are among several patently obvious selections. Appropriately cautionary in this regard is the postwar confession of Lutheran pastor Martin Niemoeller, called Hitler's favourite concentration camp prisoner. He remembered:

> First, they came for the Jews and I did not speak out – because I was not a Jew. Then, they came for the communists and I did not speak out because I was not a communist. Then, they came for the trade unionists and I did not speak out – because I was not a trade unionist. They came for me – and there was no one left to speak out for me.[1]

The time for speaking out – by all teachers and educational leaders and other citizens – is now.

Reasonable first steps are possible. Educational leaders must regain their now silent voice. Superintendents and building principals can offer vigorous public support of the balanced efforts of their school's and system's teachers. They can help illuminate the plague of consequences of a 'one size fits all' teaching procedure for reading to their community and to the nation. University administrators and professors across the campus must speak out against legislative and bureaucratic intrusion into university course content, not just in education courses, but in courses that teacher candidates take – such as history and English and mathematics. Too, as companions rather than adversaries, teachers and administrators can describe at various venues their committed practices to improve the teaching of reading. They also can draw public attention to their use of a number of research-based procedures to teach reading. This kind of joint enterprise might tout, for individual pupils and for differing lengths of time, the Success for All programme for some children, Reading Recovery for others, a strictly phonics-only programme for others, a whole-word approach for another group, a literature-based programme for still other pupils, and combinations of emphases for other children. These actions, by themselves, may help, but they likely will not be sufficient; they are beginning steps. Educators must also align themselves with other citizens for concerted political action to influence governors, legislators, and bureaucrats.

To be silent and to do nothing in this current situation is to welcome a monstrous disaster. Then, only one of the concerns will be the question: When will the phonics police come knocking?

Note

1   The University of the State of New York State Education Department, *Teaching About the Holocaust and Genocide: The Human Rights Series*, vol. 2 (Albany: New York State Education Department, Bureau of Curriculum Development, 1985), p. 313.

Source This is an edited version of an article previously published in *Journal of Curriculum Supervision*, 14(3). 1999. Reproduced by permission of the Association for Supervision and Curriculum Development.

**Extract: Dombey, H (1999) 'Towards a balanced approach to phonics teaching'.
Reading, 33(2), July, pp52-54. United Kingdom Reading Association.**

Abstract

Phonics is currently a topic attracting wide interest and concern. While there is general agreement that the teaching of reading needs to include attention to phonics, the form this should take is disputed. Recently synthetic approaches have attracted much publicity. This article examines what synthetic phonics involves, contrasting this with a more balanced approach, in terms of the phonic content taught, the means by which the teaching is transacted and its relation to other aspects of learning to read.

Introduction

Phonics has become a matter of great concern in the teaching of reading in this country. In its evaluation of the National Literacy Project, the forerunner of the National Literacy Strategy, HMI write 'The word level work caused teachers the greatest difficulty, largely because many of them did not have a sufficient knowledge and understanding of what the phonic component should be.' (Ofsted 1998, p. 9). Yet this is not for lack of materials. As well as the detailed attention to phonics included in the training programme of the National Literacy Strategy (Standards and Effectiveness Unit 1998b), the major reading schemes now include a substantial phonic element (e.g. Goswami 1996; Brown and Ruttle 1997). There are also a number of free standing phonic programmes available, some receiving heavy publicity, some accompanied by extensive rationale and explanation (e.g. Lloyd 1992; Wendon 1997; McGuinness 1998; Miskin 1998). And at least two books have recently been published that propose a systematic approach to phonics within a wider reading programme (Bielby 1998;

Dombey et al. 1998). So how are teachers to choose between all these offerings? Or is it just a matter, as the Director of the National Literacy Project suggests, of following the advice set out in the Framework for Teaching of the National Literacy Strategy (Standards and Effectiveness Unit 1998a; Stannard 1999)?

There is no doubt that in the past this topic was neglected in courses of teacher education in this country (Brooks et al. 1991). Perhaps this was because there seemed at the time to be a polar opposition between approaches to the teaching of reading primarily concerned with the construction of meaning and those primarily concerned with teaching children sound/symbol relations. While reading and learning to read were being re-conceptualised as activities involving thinking, and also the knowledge of language forms and meanings very different from those of speech, those whose prime concern was with phonics appeared to take a much narrower and less interesting view of the enterprise. Much phonic material looked unattractively old-fashioned and sounded distinctly empty and artificial.

But this situation has changed. Phonics is now widely recognised as an essential component in the teaching of reading. But why is this so? What do we mean by phonics? What do these different programmes offer? What should guide our classroom activities? These questions need to be considered. In their study of effective teachers of literacy, commissioned by the Teacher Training Agency, Medwell et al. show that in contrast to the comparison group, the effective teachers they studied had all developed a coherent philosophy of literacy teaching, based on a thorough understanding of the issues involved (Medwell et al. 1998). Effective teachers do not simply follow directions, they are reflective individuals who make principled decisions, informed by what they have read and what they have discussed on in-service courses, as well as their personal experience.

In the spirit of contributing to this process of decision making, I offer what follows as a personal interpretation. My intention is first to consider whether our children really need phonics teaching, then to weigh up the major approaches to phonics teaching in terms of their interpretation of the topic, the teaching transactions through which it takes place and the relationship – explicit or implied – between phonics teaching and other aspects of learning to read. However, it is beyond the scope of this article to look in detail at the classroom operation of these approaches.

Do our children really need to learn phonics?
Let's start with the obvious. The English writing system is alphabetic: at base it represents phonemes by graphemes – that is letters, or letter combinations. But the long and complex history of written English, pronunciation shifts not matched by spelling changes, and the importing of words from other languages together with their different spelling patterns, have all complicated the relationship between spellings and the spoken words they represent. Such common words as 'one' and 'two' pose problems for those learning to read in English, problems of a kind not encountered by children learning to read in Finnish or Spanish.

But we should not exaggerate this complexity. Letters – singly, in pairs or in larger groups – give us vital information about how words should be pronounced. With certain spectacular exceptions such as 'yacht', consonants, even in irregular words, tend to be fairly reliable. Apart from those two-timers 'c' and 'g', and with the proviso that some letters like the 't' in 'listen' may be quite silent, consonant graphemes tend to stand unambiguously for one phoneme only.

Vowels are trickier. As against the five vowels of spoken Spanish, spoken English has some twelve vowels, supplemented by eight diphthongs (such as the 'ow' sound in 'cow'). So our five vowel letters have to work overtime. The letter 'a' for example, stands for four different phonemes in such 'simple' words as 'cat', 'call', 'car' and 'cake'. As these words show, in English it is often the consonants following the vowels that tell us how they should be pronounced (Halle and Vergnaud 1980). We need to read the whole rime – the second part of the syllable from the vowel onward – if we are to pronounce the vowel appropriately. Although rimes are not totally reliable ('cow' and 'snow' are a case in point) a knowledge of key rimes, in addition to basic grapheme/ phoneme correspondences, significantly increases the decodability of English, bringing words like 'should' and 'cure' in from the wilds of unpredictability, and reducing the number of irregular words to something more manageable. English spelling is not totally erratic.

Children need to learn this, and to master the regularities and patterns of English orthography. To learn to read fluently, accurately and with the automatic word recognition that allows the reader to focus on meaning, children need a firm grasp of the patterns of grapheme/phoneme correspondences, and of the relationships between larger units of spoken speech and written text that govern most English spellings. They need grapho-phonic knowledge – that is knowledge of how letters and groups of letters relate to units of speech sound. Of course this is not all they need, but it is an essential element. A good sight vocabulary is not enough; after a certain point the limits of memory slow down expansion, and may even bring it to a halt (Byrne 1998). Without a sound working knowledge of grapho-phonics, readers have no efficient way of identifying new words or storing their existing word knowledge.

Other cueing systems cannot fully compensate for difficulty in using the information provided by the letters on the page. Semantic, syntactic and picture cues may contribute to word identification, and may be vital in disambiguating homonyms such as 'lead' or 'tear'. But they can seldom do the job of word identification on their own. Except in the most predictable contexts, letters provide essential information. Rumelhart's work over 20 years ago demonstrated convincingly that fluent reading is both top-down – involving expectations about meaning and language patterns – and bottom-up – involving the identification of words from the letters on the page (Rumelhart 1976). In fluent readers these processes operate simultaneously and interactively, so that our predictions are constrained by the letters on the page, and our application of phonic knowledge is directed by our expectation of sense. This should have forever put to flight the view that reading is essentially a top-down process – or indeed primarily a bottom-up one. Fluent reading is both, and requires the integration of complex information about meaning and language patterns with complex graphophonic information.

This much is widely agreed. Consequently it is also widely agreed that learning to read should involve attention both to the larger meanings of whole texts (including their relation to other texts and to the lived experience of the reader) and also to the 'decoding' of the letters on the page (e.g. Barrs and Thomas 1991; Beard 1993; Standards and Effectiveness Unit 1998a and b).

Do we need to teach phonics?

But does this grapho-phonic knowledge need to be taught? Don't children just work out the regularities for themselves through exposure to print? While there are documented cases of children inferring the complex relationships of our spelling system for themselves (e.g. Torrey 1973; Clark 1976; Söderbergh 1999), these appear to be exceptions, and the learning seems to take place outside an institutional setting. The vast majority of children who learn to read in school do need to be taught grapho-phonics. Without effective teaching in this area they will tend to treat our writing system as if each word were a separate logogram – an idiosyncratic assembly of letters to be memorised as a whole, not amenable to analysis – rather than a specific instance of a pattern in a system made up of interconnected patterns. So our children need to be taught grapho-phonics. But what should they be taught, how should this teaching be transacted and how should it be related to other lessons? These are the questions of the moment, exercising both professional educators and all those who have developed an anxiety about the standards our children achieve in this country.

Recently a range of 'synthetic' approaches to phonics teaching have attracted considerable publicity (e.g. McGuinness 1998; Miskin 1998; Watson and Johnston 1998). I will examine a number of these, contrasting them with what seems to me to be a more balanced approach.

What children should be taught

Synthetic phonics starts by teaching children one to one matching between graphemes and phonemes. Children are taught to tackle new words by sounding each phoneme in turn and 'blending' or synthesising the result. Proponents of synthetic approaches tend to equate mastery of the relationship between spelling patterns and their pronunciation with learning to read, as if this were all that mattered, as if on its own it could transform children into readers. There is some variation between different versions of synthetic phonics concerning what is involved. McGuinness sets out a complex catalogue that starts with one to one phoneme/grapheme relations in simple regular consonant vowel consonant (CVC) words and proceeds through initial and final consonant blends, vowel digraphs, diphthongs, spelling alternatives, multi-syllable words and finally Latin suffixes (McGuinness 1998, pp. 217–218). Others focus chiefly on the early grapheme/phoneme connections (Lloyd 1992; Wendon 1997; Miskin 1998; Watson and Johnston 1998).

But all these variants on the synthetic theme show a dominant concern with one to one grapheme/phoneme relations, with processing texts grapheme by grapheme. Indeed McGuinness asserts that this is how good readers operate: They decode text from left to right 'one sound at a time' (McGuinness 1998, p. 16). So synthetic phonics excludes the teaching of rime patterns, seeing these as confusing or insufficiently rigorous.

Yet, as I have shown, rime patterns are a key feature of English spelling: left to right, one by one grapheme/phoneme processing does not help us deal with words such as 'could' or 'dance'. If they are to learn to read flexibly and fluently, children need a more balanced approach. They need to learn of the larger orthographic patterns that govern our spelling system as well as the one to one grapheme/phoneme relations. They need to learn the rime patterns such as 'all', 'ure' and 'ould', and larger patterns such as 'ittle' and 'ation'. Such patterns are the focus of the *Rhyme and Analogy Teacher's Guide* accompanying the Oxford Reading Tree (Goswami 1996). Knowledge of these patterns will increase children's capacity to deal with new words that cannot be processed one grapheme at a time. It will also encourage them to 'chunk' sequences of grapheme/phoneme relations, enabling them to tackle new words more quickly and effectively, as Rumelhart shows skilled readers do, instead of processing them tiny bit by tiny bit (Rumelhart 1976).

Then there are the patterns that relate spelling to meaning rather than sound, operating at the level of the morpheme, the smallest unit of meaning. This takes us into word stems and their prefixes and suffixes, which may change their pronunciation in different company, but tend not to change their spelling. Perhaps the most obvious is the suffix 'ed', pronounced quite differently in 'jumped' and 'landed'. Some word stems also behave like this: 'know' on its own sounds, of course, very different from the 'know' in 'knowledge'. A balanced approach to grapho-phonics teaching needs to ensure that children learn these patterns too, as well as the patterns relating spelling to sound. The teacher's resource book that accompanies *Cambridge Reading* includes rime patterns and places considerable emphasis on chunking (Brown and Ruble 1997). Bielby's handbook *How to Teach Reading* gives full attention to all these concerns (Bielby 1998).

What I am arguing for is an inclusive approach to grapho-phonics – one that includes onset and rime and chunking, as well as one to one relationships, and also leads on to the study of morphemes. Our children need an approach that enables them to make sense of the complexities of our orthographic system, not one that denies these.

Analysis

In Davis's piece from the USA, the writer describes a frenzied political determination to implement one way of teaching reading – legislating for its implementation and consequently posing a real legal threat to those who do not abide by this view of the teaching of reading. This piece really illustrates the bitter war that some feel they need to fight in order to enforce the prioritisation of the teaching of grapho-phonic reading cues and decontextualised phonics knowledge. In my experience, teachers find this aggressive approach rather intimidating. In attempting to find out why some political factions are so rabid about phonics teaching, I am reminded of the determination of Robert Lowe in the nineteenth century in the UK to ensure that children in state schools received a certain form of literacy education in order that they did not intellectually exceed their 'betters' in the higher classes. If one is of the opinion that the basis of reading is knowing individual letter-to-sound correspondence, then early experience of learning to read may convince the child that reading *is* mainly about decoding – much more about tedious, meaningless work than pleasure. It may also mean that this is done at the expense of listening, discussing, questioning, evaluating and, most importantly, enjoying the meanings made from wonderful books. It is interesting to consider what kinds of people are produced by the two methods – active and critical, or passive and accepting.

There is a huge volume of research that looks at phonics knowledge and success in reading. Coles (2000) has shown that much of this research is not always convincing. For example, claims that phonemic awareness (hearing, distinguishing and manipulating the sounds in words) is the main causal factor in early reading achievement and the 'core deficit' in reading problems is not backed up by the research that is available. What it does show, according to Coles (2000, p1), is that:

> 'skilled readers' do better than 'less-skilled' readers only on phonemic awareness and related skills tests, but the studies show only correlation, not causation. They do not show 'how' skills and reading achievement are correlated or if some other influence – such as classroom instruction itself or pre-school literacy experience – is actually responsible for the correlation.

Dombey shows that children do need knowledge of how letters and groups of letters relate to units of speech sound. Rumelhart's (1976) work seems to show that reading needs a balance of 'top-down' and 'bottom-up' strategies – the three cueing systems that Goodman (1973) has shown – and is discussed in Hall's piece earlier in this chapter. The question remains: how should children be taught phonics? Dombey is convinced, although she does not reference any research at this point in her article, that children need to be taught phonics explicitly in schools, but in a balanced way. She writes:

> A balanced approach to phonics, therefore, involves giving children both clear and explicit instruction in sound/symbol relations and also the opportunity, demonstration and encouragement to work at the system for themselves, to perceive the patterns, make inductions about relations from particular data, and go on to draw analogies between one relationship and another. (Dombey, 1999, p56)

As Dombey shows, those who are determined to teach children using a synthetic approach (McGuinness, 1998; Miskin, 1998; Watson and Johnston, 1998) – individual letter-to-sound correspondence – create programmes with arguably strict, step-by-step sequences. Each step needs to be thoroughly taught and learned before the next is introduced and the teacher is seen as all-controlling and didactic, with the logic of the subject dominating.

I would like to see more research that demonstrates the effectiveness of teaching phonemic awareness and grapho-phonic cueing strategies in a real context, utilising literature and authentic literacy events. Children need to have the capacity to use grapho-phonic cues to read, but teachers may need always to bear in mind what the pedagogy looks like that is powered by this belief. The basics in my opinion are the pleasure, the purposefulness and the fundamental importance of story in human lives. For me this is where we must begin as, once 'hooked' on books and the reading experience, children will go on, guided by their teachers and motivated by reading's real purposefulness, to learn the skills required for competent reading. In the meantime, as far as the phonics debate goes, as Harrison (1999, p60) contends:

> In the absence of a consensus among experts, effective rhetoric and lobbying are likely to be the basis on which pedagogical decisions come to be made. What is regarded as a fact becomes a matter of belief rather than a matter of science, and accepting and rejecting a belief becomes a matter of allegiance rather than a matter of judgement.

Personal response

- Where do you stand on this issue? Do you agree with the balanced position or do you move towards the extreme?
- Find out what each political party says about the teaching of reading. Are there differences in positions from one party to another? Do you believe that their conclusions and consequently their policies are based on an informed judgement?

Practical implications and activities

With a colleague, look at a range of phonic programmes that are used in school. Do you agree with their methods? Will the children be motivated to read? Do the programmes encourage children to conceive reading to be fun, playful and about books, stories and communication? Is there a clear context to the learning that the programmes encourage?

In the next chapter we turn to issues concerning the teaching of writing.

Writing activity

Start an annotated bibliography of children's literature. You could keep this with the journal you are writing. Aim to have read and recorded 50 books by the end of your course. Make notes about the book – the themes, characters, plot and setting. Note any creative activities that come from this book.

Further reading

Department for Education and Employment (2000) *Progression in phonics*. London: DfEE

Dombey, H and Moustafa, M (eds) (1999) *Whole to part phonics*. London: Centre for Literacy in Primary Education

Graham, J and Kelly, A (1997) 'Monitoring and assessing reading', in *Reading under control: Teaching reading in the primary school* (2nd edition). London: David Fulton

4 Writing

Introduction

It was Robert Scholes (1985) who wrote that the field of English is divided into two categories of study: literature and non-literature (the former being valued, the latter being often thought beneath our notice), which is traversed and supported by another division: the production and consumption of texts. It is, for Scholes, the consumption that is privileged over the production of texts within the classroom. Scholes regrets the notion that exists in some schools that we may consume 'literature' from outside, but we cannot produce literature from inside.

> At some level we accept the myth of the ivory tower and secretly despise our own activities as trivial unless we can link them to a 'reality' outside academic life … we cannot produce literature in classes, nor can we teach its production. Instead we teach something called creative writing – the production of pseudo-literary texts. (Scholes, 1985, p5)

Scholes advocates a belief in our own worth as makers of meaning and wants a determination in schools to conceptualise the writing produced there as 'real'. School activities are not exclusively a preparation for something that commences when schooling ends. The writing that is produced in schools can contain value, richness, authenticity, beauty, depth and profundity.

Scholes would not argue that there should be no element of the academic in schoolwork. Children need to learn different skills. As he comments (1985, p8): *The writer is always reading and the reader is always writing. The student who reads the 'world' and writes about it is always sustained by other texts.* Indeed, this view will be central when we explore how children in London schools drew on other texts to nourish their creative output, in work carried out by Barrs and Cork (2001). However, the process of learning to write, like learning to read, needs to draw on the authenticity of purposeful meaning-making that reflects the practices of the outside world. Real writing – writing for real audiences – is a struggle; but the labour becomes worthwhile when the author knows that her/his work will be read, respected and valued as a genuine and authentic attempt at meaning-making. Teachers need to model writing as a process that involves composition and transcription and that often requires these two components to be nurtured separately (Graves, 1983; Smith, 1982). Writers (not all, of course) will draft their work, edit for meaning, proof-read and then publish – it is a process that requires skilled crafting. In addition, writers are often aware of their audience and the knowledge that someone will read their work motivates them. In school, the academic – the practice – and the real can deeply interpenetrate one another and many of the writers included here wish to promote this notion.

This chapter examines work that once again draws on notions of linking authenticity and the power of meaning-making with school activities. The teaching of writing is a wide area and I can not hope to cover all the important issues in this short chapter. You will need to read widely on this subject. However, I hope the issues I do raise will stimulate discussion and thinking about this vital area of literacy teaching.

We begin with Kress's (1997) view of literacy and the primacy and the essential nature of symbolic representation from early childhood onwards. Kress argues for schooling to recognise young children's skills and desire to symbolically represent aspects of their world and their fantasies using multi-modal means, and he highlights the difficulties and benefits of being given a new and complex system of signs in writing to add to their already growing repertoires of communication.

The second piece comes from the pen of one of Britain's foremost writers for children and adults: Michael Rosen (1989). In this extract he reminds his readers of the functions of writing – what it can do for writers and readers.

Finally, I have included extracts from an influential piece of research from the Centre for Literacy in Primary Education in London (Barrs and Cork, 2001) that explored the significance of linking reading with writing. All the work presented here, in its own way, makes a strong case for exploiting children's desire to represent the world and their experiences of living within it.

Signs and symbols

Paths to literacy

Before you read the next extract, read:

- Grainger, Goouch and Lambirth (2005) The 'voice strewn landscape', in *Creativity and writing: Developing voice and verve in the classroom;*
- Bearne (2002) Chapter 1 in *Making progress in writing.*

Extract: Kress, G (1997) 'Literacy, identity and futures', in *Before writing: Rethinking the paths to literacy*, pp8–10. London: Routledge.

Literacy

Questions of literacy can be dealt with in many ways: for instance, they can be thought about from a linguistic point of view by focusing on the form of language; from a historical point of view by tracing change in forms and uses of literacy; or anthropologically, by comparing literacy uses in different cultures. In educational approaches, the essential context is that of meaning-making in a social and cultural environment, together with an attempt to understand what principles children themselves use in their representation of the world. That provides the possibility of a useful understanding of the actions of children, whether as writers or readers, in their early and steadily increasing engagement with the system of writing. At the same time, it offers a possibility of understanding the characteristics of the challenges which they face in doing so. These are prerequisites for the development of new curricula of literacy, and of the teaching strategies and methods best suited for their implementation. The theoretical approach that I adopt treats meaning-making as work, as *action*, which is itself best explained in terms of the social structures and cultural systems in which children and adults act in communication.

Several points are crucial; and two are of fundamental importance. First, in learning to read and write, children come as thoroughly experienced makers of meaning, as experienced makers of signs in any medium that is to hand. The wide range of media which they employ as a matter of course – toys and constructions of various kinds; Lego blocks; cardboard boxes; blankets; chairs; corners of rooms; pens and paper; scissors, paste and paper; and so on, are not taken up in schooling in a serious fashion. In school there is instead a focus on the single medium of lettered representation: literacy. Of course, there is some attention to other forms, such as painting, drawing, building, and play of various kinds. In many classrooms there is strong encouragement of these forms. But they tend to be treated, with entirely good intentions, as *expression* of the children's feelings, desires, emotions, rather than as forms of *communication*. In any case, as children move through the years of schooling, less and less emphasis tends to be given to these forms due to the demands of the present school curriculum.

Second, in the meanings which children make, meaning and form are indistinguishable wholes. That is, the form and the material of the signs made by children are for them expressive of the meanings which they intend to make. They are, literally, full of meaning. Let me give two examples. Say children want to play 'camping' in a room in their house, and they need a 'tent'. Blankets and bedcovers draped over chairs and table provide the material and the form which sufficiently express their meaning of 'tent', at that point. Or they want to play 'pirates' and therefore need a 'pirate ship'. A cardboard box provides a container, in which they can sit, it serves as the 'vessel', and the carpet as the ocean. The material of the box and its form, suit the meaning-needs of the children at this point. In their world, form and meaning are identical. With that disposition they come to the learning of writing, a system which has all the appearances of a system of signs in which form and meaning have no intrinsic connection: the letters s h i p, for instance, do not reveal the meaning that is attached to them in this sequence unless it is pointed out.

Not surprisingly this presents some child learners with a huge barrier. I will deal with some aspects of that complex problem, focusing on the characteristics of the signs which they make, and on their disposition to signs. The question of the assumed arbitrariness of signs in writing is therefore one central issue. A second issue is that of the distinctively different grammar of speech and writing, and its effects on the learning of writing. Because my emphasis in this book is on the years *before* writing, this is less of a concern for me here, though I will mention it because it does have decisive effects on the paths into literacy, even at a very early stage. This difference is now much better understood by linguists than it was some ten to fifteen years ago, but it has not yet passed into educational common sense either in the form of pedagogies or in curricula.

My approach is to treat the children by the time they come to school as competent and practised makers of signs in many semiotic modes. The task is to attempt to understand, from that point of view, the problems they encounter in learning to write. In particular I wish to reflect on the social, cultural and cognitive implications of the transition from the rich world of meanings made in countless ways, in countless forms, in the early years of children's lives, to the much more unidimensional world of written language.

The social semiotic theory which underpins my approach insists that all signs and messages are always multimodal. That is, no sign or message ever exists in just one single mode (for instance in 'language', 'writing'). An essay written at a university is written on a particular kind of paper – hastily torn from a notebook or carefully chosen for its look or feel; it is carelessly handwritten or neatly word-processed; it is either well laid out or it is inattentive to aspects of display. It has complex grammar, or not. All of these add meaning and are inevitably a part of writing, and impinge integrally on writing.

This is especially important because we are in a period of a fundamental shift in the relative uses and valuations of writing *vis-à-vis* other forms of communication, in particular the visual. This shift has the most far-reaching effects socially, culturally and cognitively.

Analysis

Kress wants to understand children's development in writing by trying to observe which principles children use when they attempt to represent the world before school. In this way, he believes, teachers can begin to understand the challenges that children face when they arrive in school and are asked to utilise one mode of communication; yet at the same time to appreciate that meaning-making has already been part of children's lives before starting school. It is very important to acknowledge that children do come to school as *thoroughly experienced makers of meaning, as experienced makers of signs in any medium that is to hand* (Kress, 1997, p8) Basically, this means that children have been using a range of materials as signs that represent something other than the material itself. So, for example, a ballpoint pen can be a space rocket, or a cardboard box a ship. Arguably, schooling tends to forget this in its hurry to teach lettered symbols.

This view is part of Kress's perspective of the multi-modality of communication. Meaning is made by individuals using socially and culturally shaped and available resources. We communicate by means other than just writing and talk, including gaze, gesture, clothes and so on. Yet not all of these resources are recognised by controlling cultural agencies that emphasise the lettered mode. Kress highlights the tensions that exist between social agency and individual agency. So, in school, symbolic representation using letters is, arguably, the only sign-making that is truly valued socially – even artwork using images is progressively undervalued. Now, this could present a problem for children because, as Kress explains, young children's meaning-making utilises the various resources available (reflecting the multi-modality of communication in the real world). So a metaphorical connection exists for children between the form they want to represent and the material they use to do it. A cardboard box, for example, can act as a container for them to sit in as well as being a 'vessel' that they use to cross the carpet, which is, for them, the sea. Kress argues that the children see the form and meanings they wish to make as identical. With these experiences of sign-making they then are confronted with a writing system in which form and meaning have no intrinsic connection. The letters do not reveal the meaning unless you have learned to make that connection.

As children go through school, their sign-making from their early years is valued less and less and their activities with lettered symbols become the subject of more intervention and regulation by adults. The children's previous meaning-making resources are no longer given any serious communicative value by the ruling culture in which schools operate. It is, as Kress (1997, p3) goes on to say: *no wonder that the child's own semiotic disposition is not recognised in most institutional settings.* Kress wants educational institutions to understand that language is dynamic, organic and multi-modal and is constantly shaped and reshaped by those who use it everyday. He believes strongly that the experiences of the materials that children use in their early years need to be recognised as meaning-making communicative repertoires and consequently encouraged so that they can be utilised later in life. These were not the 'childish things that need to be put away', but many of these resources, Kress argues, reflect the vibrant and dynamic nature of much of the communicative repertoires used in society at large today.

There are two important points to note.

- Children come to school as experienced meaning-makers – they know about symbolic representation – and this needs to recognised and built upon.
- Ignoring these skills when forcing a new system of signs and representation upon young children may result in the failure to recognise the difficulties that they experience in the process of conversion to socially recognised literacy.

Practical implications and activities

Go into a Nursery or a Reception class and observe the independent meaning-making that is going on. What kinds of materials are being used by the children to form their meanings? How are they used and to what ends?

Next, go into a Key Stage 2 classroom. Which modes are being taught and/or encouraged now? What has been discarded?

Do you think Kress is right about which modes and materials are valued? If so, what are the signs for this?

The functions of writing

What writing can do for writers and readers

Before you read the next two extracts, read:

- Graham and Johnson (2003) *Children's writing journals*;
- Grainger, Goouch and Lambirth (2005) 'Choice and autonomy in writing', in Grainger et al *Creativity and writing: Developing voice and verve in the classroom.*

Extract: Rosen, M (1989) 'Why bother with memorable speech?', in *Did I hear you write?* (2nd edn), pp22–27. Nottingham: Five Leaves.

Having looked at some characteristics of children and some influences on them, we are now in a position to consider how writing 'memorable speech' is a worthwhile activity. However, as any writer of a text like this knows, I have a problem here in that I want to show i) how it is worthwhile, and ii) how to go about doing it, both at the same time. After all, how can I prove that it is worthwhile unless I show exactly what is involved? The 'memorable speech' activities I am referring to come later in Chapter 3 if you want to turn to them now.

I would like to isolate three characteristics of the writing process that I think are important:

i) Writing is a way of *preserving* things, or as I say to children, it's like making a photo album. Of course it's not the only way to preserve things because memory is a preserver, video and sound tapes are too. But there are unique features about writing as a preserver. The process of recording is actually quite slow, but it is cheap and portable, the direct opposite of the TV process, which is transient and disposable. When the writing concerned is personal, it has the potential of putting the writer centre-stage. It can help you deal with the world that seemingly you have little control over. A writer can play god with his/her characters in a fiction but he/she can also manipulate real people (including him/herself). Because the process of writing involves putting experience down on the space in front of you, it gives you the time and space to change what you have done. This is not merely a technical game but offers the writer the potential of seeing how writing involves selection and manipulation of experiences, thoughts and ideas. This means control and power. Writing also offers the possibility of being a 'real' activity and not a rehearsed one. This involves being authentic to one's own experience and ideas, more of which later.

Because writing preserves, it is a very convenient way to preserve the oral tradition. It can't do it with all its vigour and context, but it can do it quite well. It can record playground songs, stories my grandad told me, a tongue twister my friend told me, funny things our dads say when they stand in front of the mirror. It can represent dialect, monologue, dialogue, jokes, commands, pleadings, intimate chats and gossip. Much of this is a highly undervalued, uncherished area of human creativity. It exists as the main carrier of our culture and identity, and yet children in schools get very few chances to record it and celebrate it. (See the list on pages 15–18.) Writing it does give them that possibility.

But it is more valuable than that: because this oral output is wrapped up in personal identity, it exists in a continuum with 'personal thoughts'. If we want children to write thoughtful, authentic personal writing then they will want to be sure that we are genuinely interested in who they are. It is my experience that this involves talking and recording things like: accounts of trips to the mosque, 'how we do weddings', rules of playground games, slang words for getting told off, complaining, playing truant, being a coward, a bully etc. The act of preserving this kind of thing gives a believable context for personal writing. It also links writing about personal things to the oral power that children already possess. (See later Oral Writing.) Because I regard this continuity between the oral tradition and personal writing as being so important I have put material on this in Appendix I.

ii) Writing is a way of *reflecting* on experience and ideas. When this is personal, true experience, a unique phenomenon takes place: I put a piece of myself down on a page in front of me and I can look at it. The experience is no longer buzzing around in my head waiting to come out: it is there on the page for me to look at. And it's me! I can now make comparisons between the written experience and how I remembered it before I wrote it. I become both a participant and an observer. Paradoxically, having written about something *subjectively*, I can now be more objective about it for a moment or – as is more likely – move between the two positions: 'I did that... was I like that?... I was a fool to do that... was I fool to do that? Anyone who would do a thing like that must be a fool... I didn't think I was a fool then but I think now it was foolish of me to have done that ...' And so on.

However, to go back a bit in the actual process of writing, the very act of trying to get a remembered experience right in writing, very often involves discoveries. Most writing forces us to be linear, putting one event, thought, feeling or idea after another. Given also that the process of getting it down on the page is physically slow, what often happens is that the writer discovers aspects of the experience that lay hidden, half remembered, or unthought-out.

As a result of all these kinds of reflections the relationship between me and that experience changes. Moreover, I am partly aware that I have done the changing myself. In a very small way, I have shown to myself that the world is not simply passively received (like TV) but a place that I can help shape. All very lofty stuff, perhaps, but for me, it is the pole star I am using to guide me in what to write, why write, what to get children to write, and how to get them to write.

iii) Writing is a way of opening up a *conversation* of a specific kind because it is potentially one based on personal reflection of the kind I have just described. Of course all oral conversations can be frivolous or 'deep' as we choose. However, in classrooms, we know that it is frequently very difficult to slow things down enough to get children to reflect slowly and carefully, and then to share their reflections with each other. Sharing writing is a way of doing this. It is one way in which we can take children seriously. All those 'silly childish things' like being jealous of one's brother, or not liking housework can be dealt with as real experiences of that human stage called childhood. By treating it as real and valid now, we acknowledge that the child is not simply a pre-adult with incomplete or immature feelings. We give the child the possibility of valuing his or her own experience.

By *preserving*, *reflecting* and *opening conversations* with each other, children can begin to situate themselves in relation to each other with a lot more information. They now know, perhaps, what their grandads do, or how Sadia's mum ran away from home. At a personal level they can begin to evaluate their own experience against another person's. It is a vital part of learning 'who I am' to know 'am I the only person in the world who...?' or, as is more likely, 'you mean ... as well?' Sharing culture and sharing personal experience opens up the possibilities of cooperation, mutual respect and real friendships. It can be a strong foundation from which alternatives to 'metalanguage' can be launched.

Much of the debate about literacy is focused on the 'can' principle. 'Can he read?' 'Can she write?' I am more interested in the questions does he read, does she write? Are people who leave school, who can but don't read or write, really literate? I am interested in a practice in schools that leads people to want to read and write regardless of whether they are 'successes' or 'failures' as regards exams. With this in mind, I want in the next chapter to look a little more closely at the process of writing.

Analysis

I admit to being a great admirer of Michael Rosen. As a teacher, I would wonder at the power of his work to motivate children to 'connect' with my class and engage them in contemplation of the everyday lives of family and friends. This piece, from Rosen's excellent book *Did I hear you write?* (1989), emphasises the functions of writing. So many of us may read for pleasure, but this is not mirrored by the amount of writing for pleasure we do. This could be because we have forgotten some of the functions of writing and the experience of doing it. Like reading, writing too offers a unique experience and young writers need to know what it is. In this extract Rosen discusses its ability to preserve, to make us reflect and as a means to open conversations. Rosen contends that writing preserves fiction and experience and in so doing preserves something of the writer within its meanings. It brings power to those who write as it enables them to manipulate characters and happenings and construct them as the writer wishes them to be. Writing's power to facilitate reflection also imbues the writer with power. S/he can now look upon an experience objectively, walk round it, examine it in a year's time and think about it again. For me, even a simple activity like writing a list of things to do can bring tremendous relief from the burden of carrying this information around in my head. Imagine what relief writing can be brought from an emotional experience or event – all that thought 'buzzing around' captured for good and objectively interrogated and understood in a new way.

The real activity of writing needs to be encouraged in primary classrooms from Foundation Stage onwards. Starting with children utilising 'what is to hand' to make meaning, but later offering writing with letters and words as a powerful resource, children must be encouraged to compose. Children need to begin to manipulate words to make their own meanings. They will need to see this modelled by the wonderful books that are available for them, but also by the teacher. This will mean demonstrating the process involved and the two distinct components of writing – composition and transcription – and how they need be separated to prevent them impeding each other (Bearne, 2002). Above all they will need to be given choice of subject and form and time to craft their work for a real audience (Lambirth, 2005).

Linking reading and writing

Extract: Barrs, M and Cork, V (2001) Chapter 2 of *The reader in the writer: The links between the study of literature and writing development at Key Stage 2*, pp42–43 London: Centre for Literacy in Primary Education.

Learning to write reading
Our research supposed that reading and writing are, as Vygotsky suggests, two halves of the same process: that of 'mastering written language' (Vygotsky 1978). We expected to find young writers, in James Britton's words, 'shuttling between spoken resources and an increasing store of forms internalised from their reading' (Britton 1982). We were fascinated to observe this happening as we tracked the ways in which the two 'standard' texts that we introduced directly influenced children's writing.

But young writers are not simply learning to use written language structures, they are also learning to 'write reading' and to shape a reader's response. This is always a difficult thing to do for, as David Olson (1996) points out, written text 'preserves the words, not the voice'. The problematic task for a writer is to decide how to render what Olson terms the 'illocutionary force'; of an utterance – such features of spoken language as stress, pause, tone, pitch and intonation, which do much to affect the meaning. Alberto Manguel describes *public reading* as a form of publishing and suggests that it offers the writer an important opportunity to 'give the text a tone', something which, he implies, it is difficult to do through the written words alone.

Olson suggests that 'writing modern prose is nothing more than the attempt to control how the reader takes the text'. While we must acknowledge that this is never completely possible, we also know that good writers develop a wider repertoire of means of representing these 'illocutionary' aspects of text, ranging from the precise choice of words and the word order to the use of all the resources of punctuation and layout. It will be Rosenblatt's kind of attentive 'aesthetic' reading that will help to alert young writers to the way these features are used.

In developing their own resources, an apprentice writer's main assets will therefore be their reading and their growing sense of how experienced writers work, which skilful teaching will help them to develop, As children become more aware of themselves as both writers and readers, they begin to learn to 'read like writers' and to 'write like readers'. D.W. Harding (1963) underlines the important of this constant movement between reading and writing when he writes:

> The writer invokes the presence of the reader as he writes, the reader invokes the presence of the writer as he reads.

The internalised 'sense of the reader' is a major support to a writer in shaping a text and influences many of the choices that need to be made, from the overall style and register to the precise ordering of the material.

Conclusion

As we embarked on our investigation, we hoped to bring to bear on the evidence we gathered from classrooms, the insights from the writers and thinkers quoted above. We felt that they offered a challenging and complex account of what was involved in learning to be a responsive reader and accomplished writer of narrative.

There emerges from these sources a view of learning to write which sees it as an extension of learning spoken language. In this view, young writers become more closely attuned to the rhythms and patterns of literary language as they apprentice themselves to the experienced writers of challenging and powerful texts. Aesthetic reading helps them to attend to their own responses and to their experience of the text as a whole, as well as to its local features. Teachers develop children's responses at all of these levels, initially by their interpretations of the text as they read it aloud, and then through their orchestration of discussions of the text, which draw on the multiple responses present in any group.

This picture of what happens when we read literature in classrooms, and how these experiences can form part of the writing curriculum, foregrounds different aspects of writing narrative from those commonly emphasised in books about learning to write. It demonstrates the narrowness of preoccupations with plot, character and setting – important as these elements of narrative are. It places more emphasis on the way a story is told, on the communication of meaning, on the development of an ear for written language, and on the interaction between the writer and the reader. As we framed out research questions, planned the project, and began to interrogate the evidence, our view of the process that we were trying to track was therefore informed by the kinds of questions raised by literary theorists, as well as psychologists, educational thinkers, and experts on literacy.

Extract: Barrs, M and Cork, V (2001) Chapter 8 of *The reader in the writer: The links between the study of literature and writing development at Key Stage 2*, pp211–213 London: Centre for Literacy in Primary Education.

Research Question 2: How far do certain classroom practices support children in learning about writing from literary texts?
We drew on a number of different sources of information in order to address this question:

a) We surveyed teachers' views of their practice in teaching writing by means of a questionnaire, and followed this up with individual interviews.
b) Classroom observation enabled us to look closely at the ways in which teachers drew on literary texts in teaching writing.
c) The individual case studies enabled us to trace the effects of certain pedagogical approaches on children's progress in writing.
d) Finally, by introducing drama as a way of exploring Kevin Crossley-Holland's *The Green Children*, we were able to observe and document the impact of this kind of teaching approach on children's subsequent writing around the text.

We identified the following six approaches as being particularly effective in supporting children's learning:

i) Reading aloud was an important feature of most of the classrooms in our study
The teachers in these classrooms believed strongly in the value of continuing to read aloud to older children and regarded this as an important way in which they could bring texts alive for them and engage them with literature. In some classrooms where children were inexperienced as readers and writers, a particularly strong emphasis was put on *rereading*. Although sometimes children had copies of the text being read aloud, quite often they did not. Reading aloud seemed to be a particularly helpful way of foregrounding the tunes and rhythms of a text in a way that subsequently influenced children's writing. In most of these classrooms children were visibly engaged in reading aloud sessions. Reading aloud was a powerful prelude to the subsequent discussion of texts.

ii) Discussions around a text helped children to articulate aesthetic responses to the writing
Reading aloud sessions were generally followed by and accompanied by discussions of the text. In the majority of classrooms these discussions were very skilfully handled by

teachers, who were able to involve most of the class in responding to the text in some way. Children's initial personal responses were not cut off but were welcomed and then built on. Characteristic of the most effective practice was the way in which teachers moved children via these personal and affective responses to texts towards more aesthetic and critical responses, leading them to look more closely at what writers were doing.

iii) Drama work around texts led to strongly imagined writing in role

The drama work around *The Green Children* led to powerful writing in role in most of the classes in the project. One important feature of the drama work was the delaying of the introduction of the text itself until some aspect of the fictional world had been prefigured through drama. This had a big impact on the children, who seemed to relate much more closely and personally to this text because they had already 'lived through' some of its events and situations.

Following the drama work and the reading of the text, most children wrote in role as a character within the story. This writing in role was almost universally well done and sometimes marked a step forward in their work. Children seemed to have been helped to enter the world of the story by the role play within the drama. This piece of writing sometimes led to a shift in the case study children's writing; for instance children filled in more imagined detail around the narrative, in a way that had obviously been encouraged by the drama. Writing in role seemed to be, as already reported, a real aid to children's progress as writers.

iv) Some approaches to planning writing were especially helpful to children

Classroom observation suggested that the most effective teachers helped children to plan their writing in ways that were supportive but not overly formulaic. In general, in these classrooms, where children were offered ways of planning it was through 'open structures' which did not require them to over-plan. Sometimes 'planning' was simply done by encouraging children to reflect on and reread a text (such as the first chapter of *Fire, Bed and Bone*) which then became a starting point for their own piece of writing (for instance writing about the same situation from a different viewpoint).

v) Building in response and collaboration

Effective teachers put a great deal of emphasis on encouraging children to work on their writing together, for instance through the use of response partners or writing partners. Lessons were structured in such a way as to allow time for children to read their texts aloud to a partner, and to respond to each other's writing. The use of pairs was more common than the use of small groups for this kind of collaborative work on writing.

In the two classrooms in the study where the children's writing was particularly strong, there was less emphasis on the display and publication of children's work, and more emphasis on the sharing and discussion of their drafts and completed texts. In these classrooms a more responsive and exploratory attitude to writing was encouraged through the regular discussion of children's work in progress. 'Publishing' was more likely to take the form of public reading.

vi) Effecting 'positive transformations' in the Literacy Hour

Teachers in the project were all implementing the literacy strategy but most had some reservations about its effectiveness in relation to the teaching of writing at KS2. There was a general feeling that there was not enough time for extended writing within the Literacy Hour and in the course of the year teachers made other provision for extended writing, often establishing writers' workshops outside the hour on one or two occasions in the week. In addition, teachers continued to put emphasis on reading aloud to children, as well as on reading with a shared text. Some teachers felt there was a danger of the literacy strategy leading to a superficial approach to text work, with different texts becoming a focus in successive weeks. These teachers therefore chose to look at a few texts in more depth.

Analysis

These two pieces come from an enlightening research project carried out by the Centre for Literacy in Primary Education (CLPE), which is based in Southwark in southeast London. Colleagues at CLPE embarked on the project, which lasted a year and examined through observation and collection of case study data from five primary schools any changes that took place in children's writing when they studied challenging literature. The researchers' view was that children had to learn to read as writers and write as readers in order to produce successful and effective writing. The first extract sets out their perspectives influenced by the work of David Olson (1996), who contends that writing successful prose is all about controlling how a reader 'takes' the text. A writer needs to possess an internalised sense of a reader in order to shape a text and help influence the choices that need to be made throughout the process. The research showed – as teachers of writing in primary schools have known instinctively for many years – that good writers are also readers who absorb the 'tunes' of literature and incorporate them in their own work. This research has emphasised the crucial role played by literature in the production of good-quality writing in the classroom. It mirrors the experience of many professional acclaimed writers that reading lies behind the writing – effective writers are effective readers.

The second extract from the same book follows up, by answers, one of the key questions they had developed: *How far do certain classroom practices support children in learning about writing from literary texts?* They discovered that reading aloud, discussion, drama work, planning, collaboration and a flexible way of teaching and of organising the time, all assisted the teaching and learning of writing. I find it interesting that all of these activities are social in nature, involving talk and action with others. Following Vygotsky (1978), learning occurs in two modes of activity, firstly in the social world and then privately, in the form of individual thought. The children's exploration of the stories they were given in a variety of different social contexts facilitated the former learning to take place, leading to an internalisation of the language and the processes involved to form individual thought.

Personal response

- Think back over the last 24 hours and record all the writing you have completed. What forms of writing were they? Were they mostly non-fiction?

- Over the next month, agree with a colleague that you both will complete some form of fictional writing in order to explore the functions of writing. Perhaps it could be a short story. Explore any negative feelings you both may have about this assignment and then agree to do the task. Once it is finished, share the writing with each other and celebrate the successes.

Practical implications and activities

Ask the teachers you are working with to allow you to explore some of the techniques the teachers used in the CLPE project. It might be a good idea to begin with activities you have not seen used as often.

The next chapter explores speaking and listening and the importance of talk for learning.

Writing activity

Work with a colleague to write a review of a children's book you both have been reading. Publish this digitally, using Blackboard or some other communicating equipment – e-mail will do. Encourage your colleagues to do the same.

Further reading

Grainger, T, Goouch, K and Lambirth, A (2005a) *Creative activities for plot character and setting ages 5-7.* London: Scholastic

Grainger, T, Goouch, K and Lambirth, A (2005b) *Creative activities for plot character and setting ages 7–9.* London: Scholastic

Grainger, T, Goouch, K and Lambirth, A (2005c) *Creative activities for plot character and setting ages 9–11.* London: Scholastic

Merchant, G and Thomas, H (1999) *Picture books for the literacy hour: Activities for primary teachers.* London: David Fulton

5 Speaking and listening

By the end of this chapter you will have considered:

- **why** talk is of fundamental importance to learning;
- **what** the perspectives of social constructivism are;
- **how** teachers of English need to be aware of this area of educational theory.

Professional Standards for QTS
3.3.2b, 3.3.3

Children's literature read:
Choose two children's novels to read from Barrs and Ellis (1998) *The core booklist: A booklet to accompany 'the core book'*, or browse a bookshop or library and choose from the shelf.

Introduction

This chapter contains commentary on theories that, in my view, will have a fundamental effect upon how you intend teaching and learning to take place in your classrooms. The theory comes from two of the giants of educational psychology – Vygotsky (1978) and Bruner (1996) – thinkers that I'm sure you will already be familiar with from your learning within general professional studies programmes. They are certainly two theorists whom you must read in order to construct your own understanding of how children learn. The word 'construct', when referring to learning and knowledge, is central to the philosophy both of this chapter and, as I hope you will see, the whole of this book. Much of what is written here will have some root in 'social constructivism' – an extremely influential theory of how humans gain knowledge. The central view of this perspective is that *knowledge is made not found* (Bruner, 1996, p119) for both scientists in the laboratory and for children growing up and learning about the world around them. I'll say more about this later.

The role of talk is essential in any discussion of learning: as the authors of the following extracts make clear, it is at the root of thought. As I hope you will recognise by the end of this chapter, talk has an essential place in the classroom. In my view, a school full of consistently silent classrooms is a school where learning is a misunderstood concept.

Speaking and listening are a crucial strand to English in the National Curriculum (1999). The National Literacy Strategy (1998) does not include any objectives on speaking and listening, but recently (DfEE 2003) the Primary National Strategy has offered guidance on the teaching of speaking and listening in primary classrooms. This is a welcome development as they recommend a number of useful creative teaching methods that will encourage children to interact with one another through discussion, role-play, storytelling and drama. However, you will notice that the emphasis on much of this material is advice to teachers on assisting children 'how' to use speech effectively in different practical contexts – in other words, getting children to 'talk proper'. This is in contrast to guiding practitioners how to use talk in the classroom to power children's learning. There is a sharp difference in approach to oracy here that needs to be noted. The former is preparation for talk in society as adults and the latter is focused on talk for learning in the here and now as children. This chapter will focus mainly on the latter. My own approach ties in with the theme that runs throughout the book, drawing on children's communicative repertoires to increase meaningful learning in the classroom. Talk, in my view, is essential for children to learn generally but also to learn about language and literature and communication.

The talking classroom

Literacy and learning through talk

Before you read the next extract, read:

- Mercer (2000) 'Language as a tool for thinking', in *Words and minds: How we use language to think together.*

> **Extract: Cordon, R (2000) Chapter 1 in *Literacy and learning through talk: Strategies for the primary classroom,* pp7–10. Buckingham: Open University Press.**
>
> **The influence of Vygotsky and Bruner**
> Psychologists and educationalists, influenced particularly by Vygotsky (1978), have called for a pedagogy where discourse plays a central role in the formulation of meaning (Bruner 1986; Wood 1988; Barnes 1992). They emphasize the interrelationship between spoken language and learning and claim that discourse can enhance thinking and learning. Vygotsky made the point that thought is not merely *expressed* in words – it comes *into existence* through them. How or why talking facilitates our understanding is not clear but probably has something to do with that mysterious ability we all discover from time to time when, in trying to talk about something not yet clear to us, we find that we clarify it for ourselves and say things that we did not know we knew. As E.M. Forster is often alleged to have said, 'How do I know what I mean until I hear what I say?'
>
> Talk is a distinctly human characteristic. It begins as an unfettered chattering voice: a constant stream of consciousness inside our heads which offers an ongoing commentary and critical evaluation of life around us. When we sit quietly watching a film, or reading a book, or listening to a speech, our minds talk to us. The mind does not passively receive messages and images, it engages with them, it wrestles with them, it challenges assertions and ideas. The fact that our mouths do not always transmit our thoughts does not mean that we are not actively engaged in intellectual discourse. It is the internal voice that allows humans to go beyond the here and now, to think in abstractions, to dig out memories and project future events. This private talk was studied in the early twentieth century but largely dismissed. Behaviourist psychologists saw private speech and thinking aloud simply as inappropriate verbal behaviour that eventually disappears. Piaget (1970) referred to children's inner thoughts or private talk

as 'egocentric speech' and he distinguished this from socialized speech whose function is to communicate with others. Vygotsky, on the other hand, considered all speech to be socialized or to have a communicative function. Unlike Piaget, who considered that egocentric speech disappears as children mature, Vygotsky argued that speech turns inwards and becomes inner speech or internal language, both interacting with and influencing the thinking and learning process. He believed egocentric speech in infancy to be a precursor to internalized speech and a direct antecedent of thinking at a later stage. He claimed that, rather than disappearing as Piaget suggested, private speech continues to operate as an inner consciousness or verbal thinking. Vygotsky suggested that this internal voice enables children to comment on and explain their actions and is an essential part of their thinking and feeling. Britton (1987: 24) comments, 'It was a brilliant insight on Vygotsky's part to realise that when speech for oneself becomes internalised it is in large part because the child, in handling the freer forms of speech that constitute that mode, begins to be capable of carrying out mental operations more subtle than anything he or she can put into words'.

For Vygotsky (1978: 57), 'every function in the child's cultural development appears twice: first on the social level and later on the individual level'. This contrasts sharply with the Piagetian model of learning, where, as Bruner (1985: 26) says, 'a lone child struggles single-handed to strike some equilibrium between assimilating the world to himself or himself to the world'. Rather than seeing the child as a lone scientist, Vygotsky (1978: 26) proposed that language and thought combine to create a cognitive tool for human development and that 'children solve practical tasks with the help of their speech as well as their eyes and hands'. In focusing attention on the interaction between speech and the child's social and cultural experiences, Vygotsky provides us with a model of learning which emphasizes the role of talk and places social discourse at the centre. Most significant is the notion that children can learn effectively through interaction with a more knowledgeable other (which may be a peer or an adult). Vygotsky's influence can be seen in the work of Barnes (1976: 22), who says that 'classroom learning can best be seen as an interaction between the teacher's meanings and those of the pupils, so that what they take away is partly shared and partly unique to each of them'.

Central to Vygotsky's theory of learning is the zone of proximal development (ZPD), defined as 'the distance between the actual development level as determined by independent problem solving and the level of potential development as determined through problem solving under adult guidance or in collaboration with more capable peers' (1978: 86). It should be remembered that the ZPD is an attribute of each learning event and not an attribute of the child. Mercer and Fisher (1992: 342) point out that 'children do not carry their ZPDs with them'. Each new task will generate a different ZPD and key factors in determining children's learning 'potential' will be the nature of the discourse and the quality of teacher intervention (see Figure 1.1). Bruner (1985: 24–5) offers a useful summary of the concept:

> If the child is enabled to advance by being under the tutelage of an adult or a more competent peer, then the tutor or the aiding peer serves the learner as a vicarious form of consciousness until such a time as the learner is able to master his own action through his own consciousness and control. When the child achieves that

conscious control over a new function or conceptual system, it is then that he is able to use it as a tool. Up to that point, the tutor in effect performs the critical function of 'scaffolding' the learning task to make it possible for the child, in Vygotsky's word, to internalise external knowledge and convert it into a tool for conscious control.

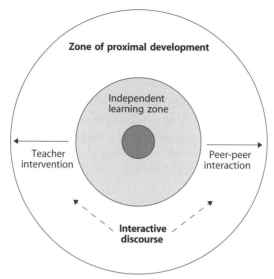

Figure 1.1. Independent and potential learning zones

The work of Bruner has been of great importance in developing our understanding of the relationship between spoken language and learning. Bruner, like Piaget, suggests the learner passes through mental development phases but argues that learning is facilitated through the provision of organized and structured learning experiences and opportunities for children to extend their current understandings. For Bruner, speech is a primary instrument of thought and the process of talking through ideas is an essential part of children's ability to handle information and make sense of new ideas and concepts. Bruner refers to this as a learner's 'channelling capacity' and argues that language helps children to code information so that cognitive restructuring can occur and a learning experience be made to fit into and extend an existing model of the world. In his later work, Bruner (1986: 127) acknowledges the importance of social interaction, negotiation and shared learning:

> Some years ago I wrote some very insistent articles about the importance of discovery learning … my model of the child in those days was very much in the tradition of the child mastering the world by representing it to himself in his own terms. In the intervening years I have come increasingly to recognise that most learning in most settings is a communal activity, a sharing of the culture. It is not just that the child must make his knowledge his own, but that he must make it his own in a community of those who share his sense of belonging to a culture. It is this that leads me to emphasise not only discovery and invention but the importance of negotiating and sharing.

Bruner, like Vygotsky, believed that learning takes place most effectively through the provision of appropriate social interactional frameworks, which he called 'scaffolding'.

Bruner illustrates this concept by looking at the way parents, through interactive discourse, support their children in undertaking tasks, initially providing substantial scaffolding and gradually withdrawing it as the child becomes increasingly proficient. In sharing a book with a child, a parent might initially look through the whole text and discuss the illustrations. The parent might then draw the child's attention to one illustration, point to the words beneath it and read them aloud. The child might then be invited to read the text along with the parent. Alongside the withdrawal of support is a gradual handing over of responsibility from parent (expert) to child (learner). Quite simply, therefore, scaffolding is a process that enables 'novices' to undertake tasks they would be unable to do independently and unaided (see Wood *et al.* 1976). The metaphor is particularly appropriate because an important feature of scaffolding is that it is gradually removed as the learner demonstrates increased competence and finally independence. Scaffolding is also highly interactive, with an onus on constant interplay between teacher and learner in the joint completion of a task, and dialogue is crucial to the process because this is how support is provided and adjusted. Interventionist techniques for developing comprehension skills and metacognition, such as reciprocal teaching, are based firmly on Vygotskian theory and notions of scaffolding, 'proleptic' teaching and the anticipation of eventual competence. Interactive discourse is a crucial element, where 'a novice is encouraged to participate in a group activity before she is able to perform unaided, the social context supporting the individual's efforts' (Palinscar and Brown 1984: 123).

Analysis

Vygotsky and Bruner were social constructivists. Constructivism takes the view that knowledge and truth are the products of human enquiry and invention rather than given directly by nature. The 'invention' of knowledge is an intriguing thought, but constructivism contends that the knowledge we possess is the result of our social inter-action with others in our culture who give our experiences of the world's meaning. Yet, knowledge can not simply be communicated or transmitted from one to another, it must be reconstructed by every learner. It is here that talk becomes essential to learning as a means to re-represent new knowledge. By doing this, knowledge can be truly discovered (Bruner, 1960). *Discovery ... is possible only by constructing understandings on the basis of extensions, elaborations or reformulations of current or preceding understandings* (Olson, 2001, p105). Knowledge is the product of 'making'. Bruner (1996, p35) writes:

> Science is not something that exists out there in nature, but ... a tool in the mind of the knower ... and you don't really ever get there unless you do it, as a learner, on your own terms. All one can do for a learner en route to her forming a view of her own is to aid and abet her on her voyage.

Constructivism states that knowledge is human made. That is to say that knowledge is not *truth* but more what is *believed* as a culture. Theories are models of things, but not necessarily the things themselves. Therefore, children's acquisition of knowledge is constructed through the reorganisation of what children already 'know' or 'believe' about the world. New concepts are matured, as Vygotsky (1978) contends, through a zone of proximal development that constitutes the 'intersubjective ground' (Olson,

2001, p107), or the path between the culture and the individual. Bruner (1983) introduced the term 'scaffolding' to describe how the mature assist the young in intellectual development. Teachers 'aid and abet' (Bruner, 1996) the intellectual development of young people by acting as instruments of culture.

So knowledge, according to this theory, is the end result of children's active interaction with human cultures. Language plays a crucial role in how knowledge is developed. As Cordon describes in the extract, language is the keeper and the arbiter of this knowledge and is internalised by the learner so as to contribute to the brain's cognitive activity – our very thoughts. Concepts are formed, organised and structured through the use of language, and learning occurs socially and then mentally. Schools can develop opportunities for talk to enable children to 'make knowledge'. Children can construct concepts and make them their own through opportunities to talk with others in their classroom and their culture. By doing so they can internalise the structures that language gives to construct new concepts. A talking classroom is a learning classroom.

Now, if all this seems very tough for you to grasp on your own, then go and talk it through with someone else. If you both still feel uncertain, then it would be sensible, given a belief in social constructivism, to talk to 'a more experienced other' – your tutor. A zone of proximal development will be established to 'aid and abet' you and your colleague to understand. Thanks to Vygotsky and Bruner's perspectives, teachers are indispensable, as they will skilfully guide you to an understanding of this concept. Learning can not be achieved in a solitary situation: there has to have been interaction with others at some time for continued intellectual development.

Personal response

- Discuss with a colleague how we talk about thinking. How do you think? What goes on in your head when you think? How much is language used? Vygotsky says we internalise our talk; are there ever times when our thoughts go the other way and are vocalised? Think about times of stress!
- Where do you stand philosophically on the social construction of knowledge? Can this be correct? Surely scientific knowledge works, aeroplanes fly safely and so on; how can knowledge be only a social construction and not necessarily mirror reality?

Practical implications and activities

Watch some Foundation Stage children engaged in some task as a group: how do they use language? Are they working socially together? Do they use egocentric speech? What are they actually saying? How do your observations correspond to the concept of social constructivism and the use of talk?

Work with a small group of children on a task. Record the session by using audio or video equipment. What is your role? How do the children respond to your teaching?

Speak for yourself

Before reading the next extract, read:

- Cordon (2000) 'The discourse of literacy', in *Literacy and learning through talk*;
- Wood (1988) 'Images of childhood and their reflection in teaching', in *How children think and learn.*

Extract: Goodwin, P (2001) 'Speak for yourself', in *The articulate classroom: talking and learning in the primary classroom*, pp26–29. London: David Fulton.

Talking, thinking and learning

Social and cognitive dimensions of talk both play vital roles in the primary classroom. Social talk involves communication between people, interacting with them at a variety of levels according to context. Cognitive talk consists of interaction of ideas – from thought to thought rather than from person to person. It calls on the ability to hypothesise, to make suppositions and to speculate. Cognitive talk is tentative, being exploratory in nature and consequently uncertain in outcome. It is not dependent on the social context but, cognitive talk, and the subsequent learning that takes place, can happen as part of any interaction as well as during those occasions when we talk to ourselves. For specific learning to take place – as in school – a social context may be contrived to encourage the individual learners within a group to articulate their learning (e.g. a seminar in higher education, preschool children at the sand tray or a small group working together in a primary classroom). Take, for example, an extract from the Cumbrian County Council video *Talking sense: oracy group work in the primary classroom*, which demonstrates the two aspects of talk, social and cognitive, in operation. The session involves four children, all under the age of seven, engaged in making individual examinations of the content of owl pellets.

Andrew:	I'm digging deep now. I'll bring this giant over … hey, this is a whopping piece of bone, isn't it? It's a whopping piece.
Emily:	I don't think it's a bone Andrew.
Andrew:	No … I'm only joking … ah … what is this?
John:	I've found a vole jaw.
Emily:	I'll see if I can …
Andrew:	What is this? What is this … is this?
Emily:	I've found some fur and it's still dry.
John:	It hasn't got any teeth on.
Emily:	No.
Sarah:	I've got two teeth.
Andrew:	Ah … aha … a limb … a limb.
Emily:	How do you know it's a limb?
Andrew:	'cause I recognise the shape … aha … oho … aha … I'm surprised the fur isn't on the outside. Are you surprised … Emily … that all the …? You would have thought that all the fur … would be on the outside, wouldn't you? But it's not. You found a piece that's still dry … it's amazing.

Both the cognitive and the social dimensions of talk are clear during this dialogue. There is no doubt that the children are interacting with each other – they give answers to questions and make comments on each other's contributions when required – but there are also times when no response is expected or necessary. Although not ostensibly talking to themselves on such occasions, the children are certainly speaking *for* themselves rather than for any social purpose. In fact, there is a remarkable similarity between the occasions when no response is necessary and the list of instances when adults talk to themselves:

- announcing intentions   *I'll bring this giant over –*
- exclamations of annoyance or delight   *Ah … aha … a limb … a limb*
- questions and answers   *What is this … is this?*
- repetition of explanations   *I'm digging deep now …*
- running commentary on activity   *I've got two teeth*
- articulating a mental activity   *I'll see if I can …*

Is this a coincidence, or is it just the way we all – young and old – talk to ourselves, both in and out of social situations when involved in cognitive tasks such as remembering, problem solving and learning? Take Andrew's contributions to the 'conversation', for example. He announces I'm digging deep now and in doing so is stating his next action and providing a running commentary on the activity in hand. It requires no response from the other children present. Andrew himself makes no immediate response to Emily's statement about finding dry fur but later his comments show that he has thought through the information she provided and had questioned it in the light of his previous knowledge: 'I'm surprised the fur isn't on the outside. Are you surprised … Emily … that all the …? You would have thought that all the fur … would be on the outside, wouldn't you? But it's not. You found a piece that's still dry … it's amazing.' His range of comments may have been similar if he had been engaged on the task alone but the contributions made by his friends enabled him to extend the content of his thinking and therefore what he says to his friends.

> Through improvised talk he can shape his ideas, modify them by listening to others, question, plan, express doubt, difficulty and confusions, experiment with new language and feel free to be tentative and incomplete. It is through talk that he comes nearer to others and with them establishes a social unit in which learning can occur and in which he can shape for public use his private and personal view. (Barnes *et al.* 1971, p. 162)

As they explore the owl pellets, the social interaction of the Cumbrian children provides them with opportunities to develop on a cognitive level by:

- trying out ideas before accepting or rejecting them;
- expressing feelings of doubt and certainty, disappointment and delight;
- giving each other support through the sharing of experience;
- reflecting on their own and each other's learning.

Their 'conversations' reflect the ways in which we all comment on experiences as they happen but in particular they demonstrate the importance of talk to learning. As the children make remarks, question and comment on their activity they are making the new knowledge their own – transforming it into words that enable them to understand new ideas.

A brief history of talking for oneself

Piaget suggested that egocentric speech is unconnected with social functions and that the learning that takes place comes about as a result of the child's interaction with the concrete world. However, noting the amount of talk that goes on between a group of children at this stage, he commented: 'True, when they are together they seem to talk to each other a great deal more than we do about what they are doing, but for the most part they are only talking to themselves' (Piaget 1959, p. 38). Using rather dismissive expressions, such as, 'True ... they seem', and 'but ... they are only', Piaget implies that the social context is unimportant. He also suggested that at the age of about seven years the need to 'talk to yourself' in this egocentric manner disappears as children become conscious of their social position and less absorbed in themselves. Vygotsky proposed a different view of egocentric speech. He saw all speech as primarily social in function, the intellect being developed within social interaction. Where Piaget says that egocentric speech disappears around the age of seven, Vygotsky believes that it changes to 'inner speech' or thought:

> Our experimental results indicate that the function of egocentric speech is similar to that of inner speech. It does not merely accompany the child's activity; it serves mental orientation, conscious understanding; it helps in overcoming difficulties; it is speech for oneself, intimately and usefully connected with the child's thinking. Its fate is very different from that described by Piaget. Egocentric speech develops along a rising, not a declining, curve; it goes through an evolution, not an involution. In the end, it becomes inner speech. (Vygotsky 1988, p. 228)

Vygotsky described a new area of understanding, just beyond the child's present knowledge, as the 'zone of proximal development'. The conversation between teacher and learners about new ideas support the learners' growing understanding. Teachers speak aloud the thought processes that enable them to understand, thus modelling the stages of thinking for their pupils. Teacher and learners act and talk together until the teacher's support is no longer needed. 'What the child can do in cooperation today he can do alone tomorrow' (Vygotsky 1988, p. 188). Vygotsky questioned the disappearance of egocentric speech, explaining how inner speech became a totally separate and differently organised language function: 'The flow of thought is not accompanied by the simultaneous unfolding of speech. The two processes are not identical, and there is no rigid correspondence between the units of thought and speech' (1988, p. 249). While there may be no 'rigid correspondence', Courtney Cazden (1988, p. 3) argues that the title of Vygotsky's book, *Thought and Language*, lost its true meaning in translation from Russian.

> We are immediately in a difficult area of relationships between thought and language, or 'thinking and speech' as the title of Vygotsky's (1962) book should be translated. The change from thought to thinking and from language to speech is more than a quibble about the correct translation from Russian. The shift in each case is to the more dynamic term: from thought as a product to thinking as a mental activity, and from language as a symbolic system to speech as the use of language in social interaction. (Cazden 1988, p. 3)

Cazden implies that active thinking is dependent on speaking aloud, not just on language used as 'inner speech'. This more active view of thinking and speaking extends the need for talking as you learn beyond the early stages of cognitive development. No matter what the age of the learner, learning is consolidated through the articulation of understanding. However, as talking aloud to yourself in the presence of potential 'listeners' can be embarrassing, learners who are socially aware alter the presentation of their spoken thoughts to accommodate an audience. They address anyone present, making tentative statements, asking questions and inviting response. Such conversations may appear social in purpose, but, as James Britton suggests of children at this stage, they are both social and cognitive at the same time:

> Obviously, a child does not give up social forms of speech when he begins to use 'speech for himself'. The two forms are at first undifferentiated, being early social speech in substance, put to two uses. But as the two become established, modification of the form takes two directions: social speech becomes better communication, while speech for oneself becomes less communicative, more individualised, better able to serve the particular purposes and interests of a particular child. (Britton 1970, p. 57)

Jerome Bruner describes how teachers provide the social framework – or 'scaffolding' – within which a learner's understanding can grow: 'Once dialogue is made possible by the child now being able to represent linguistically the aspects and elements of the operations he has mastered that he can share with an assisting adult, a powerful discourse device becomes available' (Bruner 1988, p. 94). In scaffolded conversations learners can try out ideas, make mistakes and adapt their thinking by listening to others as they work towards understanding. In the following dialogue between eight-year-old children and their teacher during a class field trip to an old, empty building, the teacher provides a 'scaffold' to learning by prompting the learners to explore new ideas.

Ann:	There's a hole.
Barry:	A chimney! A chimney!
Ann:	No – no it's for escaping.
Rajdeep:	Where's the fire?
Ann:	There isn't one.
Rajdeep:	Then why is there a chimney?
Teacher:	Could the hole have another use?
Barry:	What?
Ann:	There could be a cooker.
Teacher:	If smoke doesn't go out perhaps something comes in.
Rajdeep:	Air comes in.
Barry:	Air! Air! It's a ventilating thing …

The youngsters are prepared to offer ideas that are speculative because the social relationships between teacher and learners are secure. In their speculative remarks, the risk of failure to get the correct answer to the puzzle is a positive challenge to be overcome rather than as a confidence-sapping fullstop to learning. By questioning, stating, arguing and listening to the other members of the group the children's ideas gradually take shape around a piece of knowledge. As Barnes (1992) points out: 'The readiest way of working on understanding is often through talk, because the flexibility of speech makes it easy for us to try out new ways of arranging what we know, and easy to change them if they seem inadequate.'

Analysis

In this extract Goodwin assists this chapter in extending the argument: that talk in the classroom is essential to all learning, but that in English sessions in school, teachers can demonstrate the primacy of language to learning. Goodwin's position is that talk will assist the work that goes on in classrooms. This view draws on important elements of social constructivism theory. I intend to demonstrate in the next chapter how involving the language arts in English sessions, including drama, storytelling and poetry, exploits social opportunities for talk and facilitates the internalisation of certain creative contents and structures of oral communication.

Have you ever wondered why we ask children to discuss poetry and talk about characters in books they have read, or ask children to question events and actions that occur in plays or picture books? In some classrooms this is just the norm and the need to question why these things happen is no longer an issue. However, it should never be forgotten that all the practice in classrooms is never just 'common sense', but is always rooted in some form of theory, whether those involved are aware of it or not. Asking children to engage in 'book talk' and talk about writing is no different. To understand the desire to encourage children to talk about reading and writing is rooted in Vygotsky's (1978) theory that learning occurs first in the social context and second as thought – individually.

Goodwin illustrates the way that children and adults use talk as a tool for learning and that this talk is internalised (it disappears from the social) to become thought – often to pop up again on other occasions. By organising opportunities to use language orally in social situations about books and writing, teachers provide the content and the structure to think about these things on one's own. For example, children in a Year 4 class have been reading a poem – perhaps Peter Dixon's (Foster, 1988) 'King of the toilets'. It's a poem that wittily examines pupil disaffection in school. After a reading by the teacher, the children are asked to read it themselves and then to share a reading of the poem with a partner. They are then asked to work with their partner on formulating four questions that they wish to ask about this poem. For example, they may ask, 'why does the child in the poem choose the toilets to spend the day in rather than class?', or 'why does this child not want to be in school?', or 'why has the poet used poetry and rhyme to raise such a serious issue?' The children are then asked to take their questions to other pairs in the class to collect some 'answers', writing them down as they go. The children then share their questions and answers at the end of the session. This noisy, bustling social encounter with a poem facilitates a structure and mechanism for thinking about poetry.

According to social constructivism, the social activity with teacher, partner and other peers provides an opportunity for the content of the activity to be internalised. Ways of reading a poem, the intellectual interrogation, the questioning of others and the communal construction of meanings will form the basis of how these children can go on to read a poem independently. The structure of conversations about poetry, the vocabulary that can be used, the pleasure and the passion can all form the basis of thoughts about poetry. In addition, the way a poem can be read, modelled by the teacher, experimented with by the children can also be quietly reconstructed mentally by the children independently. A social scaffold is provided by the activity, which can be removed when children encounter literature for themselves.

Personal response

- Consider what Prue Goodwin writes about talking to one's self. Discuss with a partner when you do this. What kind of situation makes this occur? What might it indicate about theories and language?
- When you read certain books or poems, do you ever 'hear in your head' the voice of someone you have heard reading it before? Can you explain this?

Practical implications and activities

Try out the activity in the example in this chapter with some Key Stage 2 children. What is the response of the children? Do you feel there is a power to this kind of approach to learning about the pleasures of poetry?

In the next chapter I introduce the use of drama, role-play and storytelling as a manifestation of powerful uses of talk.

Writing activity

Write a short piece on one of your heroes or heroines of educational theory. Give a brief description of the person's life and a summary of their research and/or writing. Arrange a time to share your work with a partner. Encourage your partner to critique your work – they should list three positive points and three points for development.

Further reading

Bakhurst, D and Shanker, S (eds) (2001) *Jerome Bruner: Language, culture, self.* London: Sage

Benton, M and Fox, G (1985) *Teaching literature: Nine to fourteen.* Oxford: Oxford University Press

6 The language arts

By the end of this chapter you will have considered:

- **why** drama, storytelling and poetry as part of the language arts have a crucial place in primary classrooms;
- **what** kind of language art activities can be powerful in primary English sessions;
- **how** teachers can become effective storytellers and makers of meaning.

Professional Standards for QTS
3.3.2b, 3.3.3

Children's literature read:
Read some traditional stories from interesting anthologies. Try Geraldine McCaughrean's book *100 world myths and legends*, Orion (2001).

Find the work of five poets who write for children that you enjoy. Show them to your colleagues.

Introduction

This chapter illustrates just how exciting and artistic good English teaching should be. It builds on the last chapter, in particular, by highlighting how the language arts of drama and storytelling can be utilised to bring pleasure and effective learning through rich, imaginative engagement with language and stories. The chapter ends with a short piece by me on poetry which introduces the inclusive nature of one of the most respected, but neglected, language arts.

Both drama and storytelling involve oracy and vibrant opportunities for social activity that we have seen are crucial for learning. They also both draw on something that children seem to have a natural affinity with: play. Process drama invites children to construct imaginative worlds through improvisational social encounters with the teacher and their peers. This kind of play is already very familiar to children. In fact they do this all the time, slipping into imaginative worlds is part of their everyday existence. By encouraging this in school, teachers make vital connections between these imaginative experiences and the experiences that form part of other creative activities like reading and writing. Reading involves a creative engagement with the world of the story and a combining of creative capabilities of reader and author. Secondary worlds need to be formed by both author and reader, and drama activities encourage this kind of intellectual activity, often as a precursor to writing in the classroom. Drama highlights the intellectual activity that needs to be drawn from the child to both read and write. We need to give of ourselves, drawing on our own experiences and fantasies, to make meaning while reading and writing. Drama is also fun and its playfulness makes literacy sessions joyful.

Storytelling in the classroom also demands a creative engagement that is also familiar to children. As Grainger points out in one of the following extracts, storytelling helps humans make sense of their very existence and children quickly start to make stories through their play narratives.

Both drama and storytelling should always be part of a teacher's planning. The kind of risk-taking in teaching through improvised work that Grainger (in Bearne et al, 2003) discusses allows important spaces for uncertainty and, consequently, excitement. In my view, school practice should not be governed by prescription and standardisation. The teacher can model individualism and flair rather than rigid compliance through these sorties into the unknown.

The use of poetry in the classroom also offers many opportunities for social and active engagement with its many forms. Poetry has built up a reputation for children as being rather bland, boring and sometimes inaccessible (O'Brian, 1985; Dias and Hayhoe, 1988; OFSTED, 1993; QCA, 1998). However, a quick examination of the range of poetry available for children will show that poetry is none of these things. In fact poetry and rhyme play a role in all our lives everyday. My short piece on this subject asks readers to consider how ordinary and everyday our exposure to rhyme actually is.

The language arts in the classroom

Drama

Before you read the extract, read:

- Grainger and Cremin (2001) *Resourcing drama in the primary classroom 5-7*

or

- Cremin and Grainger (2001) *Resourcing drama in the primary classroom 8-11.*

Extract: Grainger, T (2003) 'Exploring the unknown: Ambiguity, interaction and meaning-making in classroom drama', in Bearne, E, Dombey, H and Grainger, T (eds) (2003) *Classroom interactions in literacy*, pp105–107. Maidenhead: Open University Press.

Introduction

In the current climate of accountability and prescribed curricula there appears to be little space for ambiguity and uncertainty. In literacy, accuracy in written construction and referential responses to text foreground much practice. Security and certainty are offered to teachers in the form of clear curriculum objectives, commonly used pedagogies (for example, shared and guided writing), and explicit assessment criteria (DfEE 1998a, 1999a). Such boundaries have created valuable shared frameworks within which the profession is expected to operate. Arguably, however, they have also limited teachers' and children's experience of ambiguity, their appreciation of multiple perspectives and alternative ways of seeing and doing.

Learning to live with ambiguity is both part of the process of working collaboratively and the process of making art (Nicholson 2000: 121). Teaching is an art form, not an exact science, and needs to remain open to the unknown, not limited by structures and strictures that prompt professionals to ask 'are we allowed?' Learning to tolerate ambiguity and uncertainty are critical life skills in a world in which technological innovations are driving rapid economic and social change. The ability to adapt to conditions of enduring unpredictability and contestability deserves the attention of educationalists. In the classroom, we should support children in handling the challenge of change and let them experience the unpredictable, preparing them for a world that cannot be anticipated; a world in which uncertainty is the norm. Their adaptability and flexibility will depend in part on their ability to appreciate multiple viewpoints, to value difference and to respond reflexively to the experience of living. These abilities are all elemental features of classroom drama.

As reader response theory suggests, all texts are open to interrogation and varied interpretations (Rosenblatt 1978), so through the exploration of literature, in storytelling and in drama, learners can develop and transform their perspectives, and learn to value those of others. Improvisational drama is a particularly rich medium for actively exploring the 'gaps in texts' (Iser 1978) in a manner which acknowledges ambiguity and leaves questions unanswered. As Moyles (1994) argues, one of the most significant attributes of play is the 'opportunity it affords for learning to live with not knowing'. In open-ended and interactive contexts in the imaginary world of drama, learners may safely experience the tension and confusion triggered by the unknown.

In this chapter I shall argue that drama, as the art form of social encounters, lives and breathes uncertainty, ambiguity and tension, and that through the adoption of different role perspectives, multiple meanings can be made. I shall explore how, through the acts of engagement and reflection, and through working alongside their teacher in role, children can come to tolerate uncertainty, trust the medium and make sense of their world. Young people need to experience the unknown in safe and supported contexts, taking risks and raising questions in order to learn to live comfortably with open-endedness and ambiguity.

Ambiguity in action
The uncertainty inherent in much drama often challenges teachers and children alike as the complex improvised experience unfolds. The risk taking required to teach drama has no doubt contributed to the primary profession's reluctance to embrace its potential, for teachers and student teachers are somewhat wary of this medium, with its connotations of theatre and performance (Wright 1999). Some professionals lack the confidence to engage fully and adopt a role and initially may prefer to employ drama conventions in the Literacy Hour, as part of shared reading or a precursor to writing for example. In this context, the teacher can safely become part of a short role play or a small group freeze frame, and extend their tolerance of uncertainty and experience of such open-ended conventions. Gradually, teachers can come to trust the art form, taking small risks and realizing that teacher in role work is not only possible, but also energizing and satisfying. Widening their experience of this tool for learning, teachers can learn to live with the relative unpredictability of drama's spontaneity and

complexity. This may be challenging, but the motivating power of drama has the capacity to enrich both children and teachers' creative potential.

In classroom drama sessions which extend well beyond a brief foray in the Literacy Hour, the class will create and inhabit fictional worlds with their teacher, adopting and sustaining various role perspectives, and investigating, questioning and reflecting upon possible meanings together. The openness that characterizes such drama, contrasts markedly with much of the current directive teaching culture, and imaginatively involves the teacher, working both inside and outside the drama. In essence, the teacher weaves the artistic experience together through employing a variety of drama conventions and building a work in the process. The skills of instruction and management are somewhat displaced in this context, by the need to negotiate and renegotiate the direction and content of the experience. While a lesson plan with learning intentions will exist, teachers in drama need to feel at ease with releasing themselves from this, in order to respond to the needs and interests of the children and to let the drama venture into unknown, but imagined territory. Teachers may deliberately choose to leave doors open in the world of drama, to ascertain areas of interest or desire and may find themselves 'raising possibilities rather than confirming probabilities' (Taylor 1995) making the situation more complex in the process. Their focus will be on the quality of the learning, ensuring that through the collaborative interaction the children are able to construct and reflect upon meaning for themselves (Booth 1989).

Analysis

In this piece Grainger encourages teachers to use drama to explore the unknown and confront the unexpected. The notion of teaching being an art form and not a direct science makes our work much more exciting and appealing.

It is important to make a distinction between two different forms of drama teaching – performance drama and process drama (O'Neill, 1995). Performance drama puts the audience at the centre of the activity. This drama is about preparing and planning performance. It may involve scripts and rehearsal. Performance drama is about plays, play scripts, assemblies and the Christmas performance. *Process drama*, on the other hand, is not audience-centred, but child-centred. The whole experience is for the benefit of the participating children. It is not aimed at a performance, but its richness lies in the process itself, the experience of going into role and making new worlds with the imagination. The work will be unscripted, improvisational and unplanned. It will involve no performance, not even to other members of the class. Of course, there will be occasions when the teacher will want one group of children to demonstrate and model good imaginative practice to the class, but once the children understand the drama you wish to create, this will no longer be necessary.

Grainger's piece argues for drama to be used to demonstrate, among other things, how there are always alternatives to readings of literature. When we read, we draw on our own experiences of life and other stories to make our individual meanings. With drama activities, children are able to enter the worlds of the texts to examine the ambiguities and uncertainties from the inside and, within the classroom, to experience literary meaning-making communally. Again, as in so much of the pedagogy this book has been championing, the social and active experience of learning comes to the fore through drama work of this nature.

In addition to its use for understanding the experience of reading, drama has also been seen to enrich writing (Pelligrini, 1984; McNaughton 1997; Booth and Neelands, 1998; Barrs and Cork, 2001; Grainger et al, 2005a, b, c). Those children who have been involved in drama activities before writing write in greater length, with greater conviction and using richer vocabulary. The writing also is often more expressive and insightful. Because drama can create more personal emotional involvement for the participating children, this effect impacts on their writing, enriching it with the children's affective engagement.

Drama is another way of validating children's own experiences, emotions and passions. Using process drama indicates a teacher's own professional approach to their role as educators. It says that teaching is not about a transmission of knowledge, but much more of a dialogue between teachers and children, where the children are listened to and respected.

Personal response

- Are you playful?
- How do you play today?
- Do you ever indulge in imaginative play? (Think carefully; I'm sure you do.)
- Discuss this with a colleague.
- How do you feel about modelling drama and role-play in the classroom?

Practical implications and activities

Go into role as characters from a book you have been reading with a colleague. Find some drama techniques and try them out in a classroom. Drawing, perhaps, on Grainger and Cremin's ideas (see the start of this chapter), try some extended drama scenarios with some children. Reflect upon its success with the class teacher.

Storytelling

Before you read the extract, read:

- Grainger (1997) *Traditional storytelling in the primary classroom.*

Extract: Grainger, T (2002) 'Crick, crack chin, my story's in', in Goodwin, P (ed) *The articulate classroom: Talking and learning in the primary classroom*, pp109–111. London: David Fulton.

Once a man, lost in the jungle for many days, caught a fever that gripped his frame so tenaciously that he grew weak and frail. He struggled feebly through the undergrowth in an almost unconscious state, until at last he collapsed. Later, it seemed to him the face of a great lion loomed over him, but then it disappeared. The lion returned however and with its huge head inclined over the man, it let a few drops of water trickle into his mouth. Every day the king of beasts brought the man water and later left pieces of fruit beside him. Eventually, the man found he could stand again, and while the lion was away he found his way back to his village.

'We thought you were dead,' cried his friends. 'Whatever happened?'

'A lion attacked me,' he replied, 'but I killed it with my bare hands. It has taken me a long time to recover.'

Three months later, the man once again adventuring in the jungle came across the lion. Silently they stared into each other's eyes. 'Take your knife,' commanded the lion, 'and cut my head.' The man did as he was bid, until blood trickled down into the lion's thick mane. The man dropped his weapon and walked slowly away.

A further three months passed and the man met the king of beasts again. 'Look at me.' demanded the lion, 'What do you see?'

'The wound on your head has healed.'

'Yes,' replied the lion, 'but the wound inside me will never heal.'

My tale I have told it, in your heart now you may hold it.

Stories and storytelling have always been used to teach about the human condition, and continue to offer teachers a rich cornucopia of delight with personal, oral, traditional and literary tales just waiting to be told. Children deserve to experience the energising nature of storytelling, the rhythms, tunes and truths of tales told and retold. Their spoken confidence and competence, their power over written narrative and their reading will all benefit if sustained opportunities to share tales of all kinds are offered. In such contexts, the classroom becomes a community of storytellers who create, investigate, shape, share, value and learn from their own and others' stories.

Storytelling is the direct and shared communication of something true about being alive. It is not only the story, but a combination of a living storyteller, situation, sound and rhythm of voice, silence, gesture, facial expressions, and response of listeners that makes it potent. (Simms 1982)

This chapter seeks to examine the significance of children's engagement in stories and storytelling, to explore support strategies for the teller, the tale and the told and to highlight the contribution that oral storytelling can make to learning in language and literacy.

Storytelling: a learning tradition

In preliterate societies, storytelling was a highly significant form of education and even in today's technological age it remains an accessible intellectual resource. The children we teach are crammed with anecdotes, hopes, warnings, explanations, jokes, family stories, reminiscences, televisual tales and tales read, heard and created which are relayed in countless conversations and playful contexts. Their humanity is expressed in the anecdotes and stories they choose to tell one another in the street, the playground, the classroom, at home and on the phone. Through telling stories, humans make sense of lived and vicarious experiences and structure their identity, since, as Hardy (1977) has argued, narrative is a primary act of mind, a mode of thinking and searching for understanding. Rosen (1988) has called it an 'irrepressible genre', a primary cognitive instrument which enables us to comprehend what events mean to us, through our inner and outer storytelling (Bruner 1986, Rosen 1984, Clandinin and Connelly 1990). In addition to its role in cognition, a correlation between early experience of story and later educational achievement has been found (Wells 1987), and the impact of young children hearing stories is widely recognised (Dombey 1988, Dickinson 1995). Through hearing stories, children learn about the features and organisation of language, and begin to assimilate and understand the more abstract mode of representing experience through writing (Wells 1987, Olson 1984).

Young children's conception of story, and how to tell a story is not only based upon the stories they have heard but also on the games they have played, the countless conversations they have taken part in, and the TV and video they have watched (Anderson and Hilton 1997). Through hearing stories and telling tales, their awareness of story, character and plot is gradually expanded into aspects of linguistic style, use of narrative technique and the syntax necessary for complex thinking (Fox 1993). Although it is undoubtedly true that children's preschool experience and cultural use of story differs (Brice-Heath 1983, Minns 1990), storytelling is a general language habit, and thinking through story remains a universal human competence, which can be developed and refined in school (Egan 1988, Bage 1999). 'We need to learn strategies of narration when we are very young in order to grasp that we can become our own narrators, the storytellers of our lives' (Zipes 1995).

Stories play a critical role in self-creation as well as self-discovery, so no one need be a prisoner of their own autobiography, at least from a constructivist viewpoint. Furthermore, if we are to work *with children* in our classrooms, and not merely deliver prescribed curricula to *pupils*, then opportunities to value their own lives, their stories and cultural experience need to be created and built upon in the classroom. Narrative plays an important part in both cognitive and emotional development and needs to be recognised more fully as a tool for learning, right across the primary years. Narrative thought is supported not only by literature based classrooms, but by a range of classroom contexts such as play, drama and storytelling, all of which contribute effectively and affectively to children's oral and literate development, building their sense of self and expanding their imaginative capacity. When a storytelling ethos is established and the oral and literary traditions are both valued, then the National Curriculum (DfEE 1999) requirement to integrate the three language modes can be fully realised. But in order to achieve this successfully, the tale, the teller and the told, must all work in harmony (Colwell 1991, Medlicott 1989).

Analysis

We know that stories provide a major way to understand the world (Wells, 1981). Through storytelling we have all made order out of chaos and uncertainty of our human condition. It has a fundamental place in all our lives. Children, from an early age, are full of anecdote and story and show considerable implicit understanding of narrative structures, plot lines and linguistic styles (Fox, 1993). When children are asked to tell stories in the classroom they begin to build on these skills and start to take notice of the needs of their live audience during composition. Working in these social contexts assists learning about writing for unknown distant audiences and children begin to 'write as readers' (Barrs and Cork, 2001), having internalised the lessons of the parallel oral experiences. Orally, the dramatic aspects of story are highlighted as children explore the use of voice and body to tell the tale with passion. Bearne (2002, p99) has written: *lessons learned through face-to-face engagement, through the use of spoken voice can then be directed towards developing a secure written voice.*

Traditional tales are often used by teachers to introduce oral storytelling to children. Their origins are part of the oral tradition so they often have strong story lines and memorable narrative structures. By asking children to learn and retell these kinds of stories they can act as a scaffold to a greater understanding of these crucial linguistic and literary features (Frater, 2000). The experience of telling tales to live audiences and employing oral compositional features can be internalised by young writers to assist them in their own individual work. Recording and reflecting upon the lyrical phrasing, the structures and literary language of oral work can develop the children's awareness of the role of language in shaping a story (Grainger et al, 2005d).

Personal stories can also be used for oral storytelling. By drawing on their own lives, children are provided with the content of their stories. As we saw in the earlier chapter on writing, retelling one's own life through storytelling also means being able to take control over it psychologically.

Children can experience power over language when they tell tales. They can see the effect upon their audience, experiencing the emotional impact and the enormous appreciation received after a successful retelling. Teachers can model storytelling. You will need to learn some good stories, internalising them, personalising them and taking ownership over your versions. You will be amazed by the difference in impact of a story 'told' compared with a story 'read'.

Personal response

- Draw a timeline of your life from 18 years old until now. Mark four significant happenings in your life on it. For example, it may be passing your driving test, the birth of a child, marriage, passing an exam, buying a house, and so on.
- With a partner, decide which one you will retell as a simple story. Tell it to your partner and afterwards tell the tale another three times to three different people.
- Now try writing it down as you told it.
- Discuss the whole process with someone. Did the writing come easier?

Practical implications and activities

Learn a tale to tell a group of children. To help you, draw round your hand on a piece of paper. On the thumb write or sketch the start of the tale. On the following three fingers write or sketch the next key events in the story. On the small finger write or sketch the conclusion. Use the 'storyhand' to help you retell the tale. Tell it to yourself, then a colleague or a loved one, and then try it in a class to children.

Reflect on:
- the experience – what was happening in your head?
- the response of the children;
- the use of language.

Poetry

Lambirth, A. (2002) Introduction, in *Poetry matters,* pp1–3. Royston: United Kingdom Literacy Association.

Poetry matters
Poetry matters every day. The essence of poetry, its heart, its pulse seems to follow us around everywhere we go. We can be seen tapping out its rhythms with feet, fingers, pens and pencils everyday. When we play with words in jest, love or spite we use the tools and techniques that poets through the ages have utilised to make their 'verbal music'.

It is in no way exclusive and in every way inclusive. We can hear it everywhere we go, including: the football terraces, the playground, the church, the mosque, the building site, the university and the primary school. It is there in many parts of our day: before bed, in bed, breakfast time, work time and play time. In truth, it is difficult to think of a time or a place when words are never used in special ways; when we do not play with words and their meanings, or create rhyme or verse, or carefully put words together in an order that sounds right and heightens our meaning making. We hear it in many guises including pop song, opera, joke, chant, jingle, sonnet, rap, nursery rhyme and so on. Some we love and are moved by in the deepest ways, others we want to curse and call shallow and dull, but always there is an affect. All of these forms belong to a family called poetry.

Poetry and playfulness
Playing with language to enhance our meaning making comes early. Children enjoy doing this whenever they are together. It prompts laughter and tears and is a powerful part of our communicating repertoires. The point here, is that right from the start of our linguistic histories we understand how to enhance the meanings we wish to make. Young children appreciate this kind of language when they hear it. Primary school teachers soon become aware of the influential characters in their class by the power of their ludic use of language. Poetry, as it has been written through history, also 'plays' with words and structures and manipulates them to enhance meanings, sometimes, in the most profound ways. This is the pinnacle of this early play with language and

suggests that it is crucial to build on the early enjoyment of the manipulation of words for effect. David Crystal (1998) contends that it is healthy and 'normal to be (linguistically) abnormal by engaging in language play' (p58)

Children and poetry

Children use rhyme and verse to skip, clap and dance to. Their movement to the beat of this verse is intrinsic to their play and their enjoyment of this form of language. They seem to share with some of the world's poets, past and present, the pleasure of the 'taste' and tingle of delicious and strange sensations of words on their tongues and the effect of rhythm on their bodies. With so much implicit understanding of this world of verse and rhyme, the potential to build upon these foundations looks limitless.

Poetry and rhyme are so inclusive that it seems that we sometimes fail to recognise them when we hear them and miss how fundamental they are to our every day experience of the world. It is important to remind us of our understanding and ability to utilise their techniques.

Anxieties

If poetry and rhyme are part of our everyday experience it does seem strange that the area of literature called 'poetry' often causes so much uneasiness in adults when they are asked to read, write or discuss it. Poetry seems to be the most neglected form of literature in terms of adult readership. These days, primary school teachers will know the popularity in their classrooms of poetry written for children, but this enthusiasm for verse seems to be extinguished later in life. So, something must happen – could it be schools and the nature of the approach to poetry in these institutions?

This book invites teachers to reflect upon their own knowledge of poetry and rhyme and then ask children to do so as well. When we recognise their fundamental inclusion in our own experience, we can go on to examine the work of others who have learned how to explicitly utilise them for different purposes and audiences. It is hoped that building on these foundations, teachers and children will feel more confident to enjoy poetry and be convinced of its potential as one of the most important, profound and powerful means of communication between individuals.

Poetry for learning

The benefits of using poetry in the classroom are astounding. It may be useful here to remind us of some of them. Firstly, its ability to generate delight means it is a great motivator for encouraging reading. It has the capability of changing children's crucial attitudes to reading by drawing on children's interest in word play. The wealth of verse published by our modern poets seems to be able to tap into children's humour and experience of life at their level. Children adore the work of Michael Rosen, Brian Patten and Roger McGough, to name but three, and will want to hear it again and again. Secondly, research informs us (Bryant and Bradley, 1985) that children who are exposed to rhyme and alliteration from an early age develop a greater phonological awareness, contributing directly to the learning of strategies readers need to employ. In addition to this, we know it encourages concentration and listening skills; it also helps develop literal and inferential comprehension and response. The writing of poetry, with its emphasis on vocabulary and heightened language use can only help develop the writer's ability to experiment with the potency of written forms. Children who are encouraged to write poetry also become involved in a process of self-discovery – it assists children in understanding their experiences of everyday life.

Analysis

All of the language arts that have been discussed in this chapter have involved playfulness. Poetry is no different. This short piece, which acts as an introduction to a practical book (Lambirth, 2002) on teaching poetry, highlights poetry's inclusive nature. Heightened forms of meaning-making can be heard in many different settings and, like the poetry found in books, is sometimes beautiful and sometimes ugly. When we play with words at home, at work or in the street we are engaging in similar activities to professional poets – we mess around with words and their sounds for effect. This is not unusual and it is certainly not elitist; it is just 'normal' (Crystal, 1998). Yet, as this extract points out, anxieties can form around the teaching and learning of poetry. This may come from our own experiences as children in school, where often poetry was just the 'stuff' of exams. The good news is that we no longer have to feel this way. There is now so much poetry available for children to suit all tastes that no one needs to miss out on this vital form of writing.

Children's first encounters with language are frequently poetic in nature, as caregivers provide food, take the child to bed or bath them with the accompaniment of song or rhyme. In later years the culture of childhood is alive with poetic language through songs, chants, playground rhymes and advertising jingles. Teachers can nurture children's affinity with rhyme by building on this implicit knowledge of poetry.

Children come to school knowing and understanding the multi-modal nature of poetry – its close affinity with music, movement and dance. Indeed, children come to us with the music and movement of poetry reverberating inside them. They are aware that poems are alive and free and children know little or nothing of their confinement on the page. Schools inform them of that. Yet, schools do not need to introduce poetry like this. The role of the teacher is to keep poetry dynamic and vibrant, releasing it off the page at every opportunity. The singing, the dancing and the movement need to continue.

Like children, we too know about rhyme, poetry, dance and song. Poetry needs us to save it from a lifetime on the page. Teachers need to feel empowered to bring life to poetry by drawing on children's love of playfulness and playing with words.

Personal response

- Find some poetry books for children and adults. Find time to read some and show the ones you enjoy to colleagues. Read them aloud.
- Discuss with a colleague your background in poetry.
- Tell a colleague a rhyme or a poem you know from your childhood. Naughty ones are fine!

> ### Practical implications and activities
>
> Find some poems that you would like to introduce to the class. Ask the children in groups to perform the poems using props, voices, movement or any ways to bring the poem to life.
>
> Reflect upon how the children responded.

In the next chapter I introduce some issues concerning assessment.

Writing activity

Try writing a poem on a subject of your choice and in a style of your choice. Immerse yourself in poetry first. Read some poems aloud, study the subjects of the poems and have a go yourself. Discuss your ideas with a colleague and ask for feedback on your efforts.

Further reading

Barrs, M and Rosen, M (eds) (1997) *A year with poetry.* London: Centre for Literacy in Primary Education

Sedgwick, F (1997) *Read my mind: Young children, poetry and learning.* London: Routledge

Wilson, A with Hughes, S (eds) (1998) *The poetry book for primary schools.* London: The Poetry Society

7 Some perspectives on assessment

By the end of this chapter you will have considered:

- **why** issues around assessment are crucial for teachers to understand;
- **how** teachers can apply socio-cultural perspectives to judgements about children's development in literacy;
- **what** measures can be taken to use assessment for the benefit of the children in your class.

Professional Standards for QTS
3.2.1–3.2.7

Children's literature read:
Read the work of writers and poets for children or adults who write in non-standard English. For example, James Berry's *A thief in the village and other stories*, published by Puffin (1989); Jackie Kay's *Two's company*, published by Puffin (1992); Grace Nichols' (ed) *Can I buy a slice of the sky?*, published by Hodder Knight (1991).

Introduction

As in all the chapters in this book, I want this one to encourage you to think about particular issues around the subject it offers; and like all the other chapters, I have had to choose from a vast range of important issues to find one or two on which to concentrate. I can not hope to cover all aspects and issues, so I hope that the ones I have chosen will stimulate debate and motivate you to read further into the subject. I have included issues that maintain the theme of authenticity of literacy events in school. Reading assessment is examined through the 'lens' of socio-cultural theory; the assessment of writing and speaking and listening asks teachers to consider a meaning-related approach.

The importance of the way teachers assess children can not be overstated. These ways will influence how children perceive themselves as readers, writers, talkers and people and will consequently influence the direction children will go through education. It has been argued that since the advent of the National Curriculum, the way teachers have been asked to assess literacy has become *increasingly circumscribed within a narrowly mechanistic framework* (D'Arcy, 1999, p3) that pays little attention to children's meaning-making in reading, writing, speaking and listening – with too much emphasis on the 'correct use' of language in inauthentic conditions. Much of the work presented in this book constructs children as active meaning-makers whose home literacy events as well as school's need to be considered in a positive way. This book has raised issues of culture and its connection with literacy practices and has considered the differences between school and home cultures. A monocultural assessment of particular literacy practices will not consider, nor think important, the meaning-making of cultural communities other than those valued by school. Arguably, the National Curriculum (1999) and the National Literacy Strategy (1998) and assessment by National Tests take little interest in children's cultural background (Jones, 2003).

The need to conform to a singular literacy practice in school compels teachers to ignore cultural input from the children in the classroom, closing down opportunities for the dialogue between children and teachers discussed elsewhere in this book. I want you to consider some of these issues in this chapter. However, as I have said before, beware of my own beliefs that have inevitably influenced my choice of contributors. Take a critical perspective, read around the subject, talk to colleagues and build your own informed professional opinions.

The first piece of work concentrates on the assessment of reading. I draw once again on Hall's (2003) book on reading assessment, *Listening to Stephen read.* I have used a very short extract from Mary Hilton's discussion of Stephen's reading progress to high-light a socio-cultural perspective on assessment of reading and literacy.

The second short extract draws on Pat D'Arcy's work on contrasting paradigms for assessment of writing. It offers a perspective that concentrates much more on the process of writing and children's authentic attempts at meaning-making.

The last extract comes from the 1990s – the National Oracy Project. I want you to read this more practical extract bearing in mind all the work this book has highlighted, in order to try to identify significant connections.

Perspectives on assessment

Assessment of reading

Before you read the extract, read:

- Graham and Kelly (2000) 'Monitoring and assessing reading', Chapter 4 in *Reading under control: Teaching reading in the primary school.*

Extract: Hall, K (2003) 'Mary Hilton's perspective', in *Listening to Stephen read: Multiple perspectives on literacy*, pp126–128. Buckingham: Open University Press.

KH: *Thanks for that Mary. What would you like to know about him as a reader?*

MH: I would like to know a lot more about him than the evidence from the video and miscue. I would like to know what he reads – and I'm taking reading in a very broad sense. I would like to know what he reads for pleasure, and if that's video text. Does he play computer games? Does he watch videos? What other texts does he approach? What does he genuinely choose for himself? What are his real likes and dislikes? This might take a lot of working with him to determine that, and indeed watching him and talking to his parents.

I would like to know a lot more socio-cultural information. I would like to know who he plays with, what the reading practices at home are, who reads what and who gets

---

pleasure from what, what the kind of literacy practices are, who writes what and so on – information that could be gleaned from his parents, possibly not. I'd like to have a much wider frame than the evidence of him performing on a miscue or a taped thing like that. I'd like to know what he writes too. I'd like to see examples of his writing, right from the early stages, and to see developmentally how he's going along with writing.

I'd really like to know from him as well what he thinks it means to read, what he sees reading is for, if you like, and what he understands about the nature of reading. And I'd like to know how that's contextualized within the culture of home and the community. And so I'd also like to know what his friends get up to, what they read, and what they talk about as I just don't see how you can move him onwards with reading in any way without having a lot of that information to hand. You can then get him stimulated and I think that's what I was very worried about when I watched the video. I've called it a pathology of school. What was happening was that there seemed to be a school-level definition of reading that he was attempting to come up to but it wasn't a real level, no personal autonomy involved in any sense. His own sense of his personhood if you like wasn't there and my worry is there will come a widening gap between those two things – school literacy and a literacy that is personally meaningful to him.

KH: *Many thanks for that Mary. What do you think his teacher should do to advance him as a reader?*

MH: I think there were a lot of things his teacher could do. It sounds a bit bossy but I think she does need to review her whole classroom practice. I think she is caught into a paradigm that she would need to break out of which involves certain kinds of rather rigid definitions of what reading is. I think she's got to have a wider and more imaginative classroom literacy practice. She needs to bring in more texts that those children, who are failing, are interested in. I think she needs to introduce more media and more popular culture into her work – so that's taking a wide-angle look. In more detail, she needs to talk in depth to his parents about his reading habits – when he does read, who to, what he reads, through to how the family view reading so she can work her practice in more culturally sympathetic kinds of ways.

Then there are also important facets to getting him to write as well as to read, so getting him to write about things that give him pleasure, getting him to re-engage with the processes of literacy along pleasurable lines. It seemed as if he was doing it for her, and probably because his parents were anxious; it wasn't engaging for him though. I think she needs to work very hard at re-engaging his interests, and his imagination, through following his interests. She needs to bring to the classroom those kinds of texts that interest him. She needs to engage him in ways that he finds meaningful. That might well mean making overheads for a little media production or writing texts for his friends, or setting down to write a fantasy story that he really can deeply engage with through play and through his imagination. And so I think there are quite a lot of things she could do.

I'm sorry to go on at quite a general level as I'm not sure what she really does do but those are the kinds of things that I would do.

And my absolute aim would be to get that child hooked on books and I wouldn't really care too much what those books were at this stage; I'd want him to come to literacy as a meaningful activity.

It seems the teacher does have comics in the classroom but clearly that's not quite enough and I don't blame any teacher, particularly inexperienced ones, as they've been trained to disengage with more imaginative approaches to the teaching of reading. I have the impression that his teacher may be of the view that you can train pupils through phonics, exercises, and instruction. Of course you only do learn to read at a very basic level with those kinds of techniques, and if you want children to read at a deeper level, you must bring back in practices which promote autonomy and pleasure. If you want children to understand inference for example, you must do this to engage with texts in an intense and meaningful way.

I've jotted down things like computer games, what stories turned him on, what reading does he do for pleasure, home-school links and all the kinds of changes in classroom practice that that might incur. To re-engage this child with meaningful literate practice is key.

Analysis

One's own view of literacy and reading will colour the approach to be taken with assessing children's development. Hall's book illustrates the multiple perspectives on assessment that different scholars have taken. She asks a number of different academics to comment and make suggestions for ways of assisting a child to read. In this extract Mary Hilton is discussing the reading development of a child called Stephen. She has been shown video footage of the child reading and the results of a miscue analysis. Miscue analysis examines the child's 'mistakes', or 'miscues', when reading. In doing this, teachers can identify the cueing systems the child is using. This method comes originally from psycholinguistic perspectives developed by Goodman (1986). However, Hilton expresses the need to learn more and, significantly, different forms of information about the child. She is also concerned that the books that the child is offered do not appeal to him. She describes the choice of books as 'artificial' and Stephen's reading as showing signs of no commitment, which is also significant in terms of Hilton's view of reading and the reading process. She goes on to say that the information she needs includes evidence of what Stephen does enjoy reading, the kinds of texts (including video, film and other screen-based sources), the nature of reading practices he has, who he reads with and when. There is an appeal from Hilton for a more authentic understanding of Stephen's literacy experiences in the real world outside school.

You will notice that the concept of 'reading' is widened to include the reading of texts other than books and the written word. This kind of information is socio-cultural in nature. It's a perspective we have come across before in this book. Hilton is much more concerned with cultural practice than personal skills; there is a shift from emphasis on the individual to the social and cultural context in which literacy occurs.

In order to understand Hilton's position, you may need to go back to earlier chapters in this book to look again at socio-cultural perspectives. An important aspect of these perspectives is that instead of assessment ignoring, or treating as a deficit, children's literacy experiences from their home cultures, attention needs to be shifted to the possibilities offered by such experiences. Miscue analysis only picks out the skills associated with one kind of 'literacy club' (Smith, 1978) – an elite club only open to those who indulge in a particular form of literacy. For Hilton, assessment must include, at least, a knowledge of children's home literacy practices so as to understand how children interact with literacy events encouraged at school. Yet clearly, formal and high-stakes testing like National Tests and later GCSE assessment make no real attempt to validate other forms of literacy activity.

We have seen earlier in this book how ignoring home cultural literacy practices can lead to disaffection through alienation from the curriculum and the potential for underachievement. This is a serious issue for society and one that, arguably, governments have failed to address.

Personal response

- Consider the socio-cultural perspectives within this book as a whole. Discuss with a group of colleagues how this perspective will influence your assessment of children in your class.
- Consider how the curriculum and consequently assessment would need to change so as to fully incorporate and appreciate the reading practices in different social environments.
- How could a government legislate for such a change? Whom might this change affect and who might object?

Practical implications and activities

Carry out a miscue analysis or running record as described by Graham and Kelly (2000). Then talk to the child about reading at home. Ensure that you broaden your perspectives of the notion of reading – include screen-based reading. How do teachers find out about home literacies? Discuss this with a teacher.

Discuss your results with a group of colleagues. What aspect of your assessment has been of most use and why?

What would you do to address this child's needs? What kind of changes would you make to the reading practice in the class and for this child?

Assessment of writing

Before you read the extract, read:

- Bearne (2002) 'Assessment of writing', in *Making progress in writing*;
- DfEE (1999) *National Curriculum Attainment Targets for English Key Stage 1 and 2.*

Extract: D'Arcy, P (1999) Part 2, in *Two contrasting paradigms for the teaching and the assessment of writing: A critique of current approaches in the NC*, pp48–49. Loughborough: NATE.

Responding interpretively to a pupil's story
Guidelines for teachers

First response
Engagement: Internalising the story

Focus on what you are 'making' of the story inside your own head. What thoughts, feelings, visual impressions come into your mind as you read? Look through the words on the page to the meanings they evoke for you.

Second response
Appreciation: considering the writer's achievements

Consider how the way in which the story was written enabled you to engage with it meaningfully. Think about those aspects of the writer's handling of the narrative which were helpful to you as a reader, such as sense of place, insights into how characters behave, creation of suspense or atmosphere, convincing narrative voice. In your interpretive assessment relate your comments to specific details which look inwards to the effect which they had on your imagination as you read the story. Avoid generalisations.

If the story failed to engage you imaginatively, explain what the problems were, for you as a reader, such as a lack of any sense of engagement on the part of the writer, insufficient detail, lack of coherence.

Analysis

In this very short extract D'Arcy urges teachers to engage with the writing that is to be assessed in the same way one would engage with a professional piece of writing from a book. She takes a more authentic approach to assessing writing. Her view is that official publications relating to the teaching and assessment of writing use a *narrowly linguistic paradigm* (D'Arcy, 1999, p49). For D'Arcy, this documentation, which includes the English orders and the criteria for assessment for SATs (National Tests), gives no genuine recognition that writing is a mental activity before it becomes a text. Officially, assessment is almost solely concerned with the child's writing as an object for linguistic analysis at the expense of consideration of meaning that all texts produced by writers seek to convey.

D'Arcy (1999, p50) contends that in official publications on writing assessment: *There is no reference … to writing 'from the inside', from the reservoir of recollections and speculations which are already a part of children's lives, related to their cultural experiences and to the values they hold.* She asks teachers to read children's work as the writing of human beings in the 'here and now', work that seeks to make meaning from their place in the world. In a sense, she asks teachers to read children's work as they would any form of writing, professional or otherwise – as a genuine piece of authentic meaning-making. Here, I'm reminded of Robert Scholes's work that I discussed in the chapter on writing. This perspective wants the academic (the practice and learning about the craft) and the authentic to interpenetrate. A focus on the language alone will remain meaningless unless there is greater acknowledgement of the semantics involved.

Earlier in her book, D'Arcy explains her perspectives about learning to write. In doing so she quotes Mayher et al (1983) concerning the connection between fluency, clarity and correctness. It is worth quoting from here (p97):

> The best way to understand and encourage interaction between the child's growing linguistic system and her emerging ability to write is to see the latter as a developmental process, which first emphasises fluency, then clarity, and finally correctness. In stressing fluency, the goal is to build a sense of comfort, confidence and control in the growing writer. Young writers must feel that they have ideas and a language system in their heads and that they can combine these to fill up blank sheets of paper.

As D'Arcy says, if teachers are pressured by assessment that highlights correctness and clarity first at the expense of fluency, then a child's belief in their ability to express an individual voice is threatened.

Personal response

- After reading the attainment targets and exploring official criteria for assessment, consider D'Arcy's view. Do you agree with her, or are there aspects of her views that you do not agree with?
- Discuss this approach to assessment with a teacher and another colleague on your course.

Practical implications and activities

Find some children's writing and assess it from different perspectives.

Level the work using the National Curriculum criteria used for National Tests.

Now, assess the work using the method that D'Arcy uses. Draw on Eve Bearne's (2002) writing miscue analysis from her book *Making progress in writing*.

Which methods provided you with the best assessment of the child's work and would assist you in teaching this child?

Assessment of talk

Before you read the next extract, read:

- Mercer (2000) 'Development through dialogue', Chapter 6 in *Words and minds: How we use language to think together*;
- Grugeon et al (1999) 'Monitoring and assessing speaking and listening in the classroom', Chapter 6 in *Teaching speaking and listening in the primary school*.

Extract: National Oracy Project (1991) Chapter 10 in *Teaching talking and learning in Key Stage 2*, pp57–58. York: National Curriculum Council.

Assessment

'What the Oracy Project has meant for me so far is that planning for talk, enabling it to happen in my classrooms, observing my children talking, have all become a way of working for me, not something extra I impose on myself.' (An Oracy Project teacher)

Talking, and the content and purpose of talk, are part of the same process. Talk is not a discrete skill that needs repetitive practice in the same way as learning to swim, or to play an instrument. As talk is used to approach and express understanding in a range of curriculum areas, so talk itself is developed and refined to fulfil its purpose. We need to set up situations in which children can succeed, to prompt and encourage that success, and to feed it back to the child in order to confirm what he or she has probably already sensed.

All the time that teachers are with children, they are listening, watching, noting what children are doing and saying, and using this in the judgements they make about what children are delivering, and what opportunities need to be created for them. Sometimes this leads to an immediate response, sometimes it is simply noted and recalled in future decisions. Collecting information about the children's learning, however informally, provides the resource on which teachers draw in their personal reflection and public recording. It is this continual process of noting and responding to children's talk that is now recognised as assessment in practice.

Assessment has been defined in two ways:

– as a means of becoming informed about a child's level of competence;
– as a means by which the quality of learning and teaching can regularly be monitored.

A notion of assessment needs to accept these and to go beyond them. We tend to see it as embracing all those strategies – continuous strategies – through which we become more able to provide:

– relevant learning experiences for the child
– more effective insights into the quality of our own teaching
– more useful, and contextualised, information for others.

The Project also sees assessment as a process which involves the children themselves, a partnership which not only assumes a quality of relationship, but contributes to it. There are some aspects of the assessment of talk which have, quite legitimately, concerned teachers from the outset. Here are some of them:

Why is it important to find ways of noting children's talk?
- Because it can inform you of the effects of your present practice, and indicate areas for future planning.
- Because it can show you what children understand, and how they go about using talk to achieve understanding.

- Because it can enable you to support your views about children with evidence from what they do and say.

How can I assess children at their best?

Children are using talk in different ways and for different purposes all the time that they are speaking and listening to others. How can you, the teacher, even begin to capture them all? There are also times when their interest and enthusiasm may have come alive, and their involvement in their use of talk may be particularly concentrated. It is impossible to be sure that you are around when it happens, and therefore what you have noted may not be the truth about a child's real competence. This is why your monitoring of children talk can only be a process of sampling. It is also why that sampling needs to be regular, so that, over time, a profile can emerge of what a child habitually does in speaking and listening.

How do I know what talk is better than other talk?

Because of the variables which affect talk, and because language development is not a linear process, it is not possible to make absolute judgements in this area. Yet you can note children's success, in explaining, supporting others, listening and responding, using questions, summarising a group discussion, seeking consensus, and so on. It is important to be able to support your comments on such achievements with references to, quotations from, or indications of, the events which took place.

How valid is my own judgement?

The teacher's judgement, as a trained professional, is not only legitimate, but essential. As the person who will spend the longest continual time in contact with the child as learner, your experience of the child's development is unique. The whole role of the teacher involves the use of informed sensitivity, and the constant process of assessing situations and responding to them. Your judgement therefore becomes a statement based upon your own experience of a child's learning, and your evidence will be the information you have collected in the course of your daily interaction with, and observation of, the children.

What should I be looking out for?

Now that 'Speaking and Listening' as a profile component in English has been given a status equal to reading and writing, you will need to reflect this in your interest in the children's progress. The problem is, what should you look for? It is tempting to read up some authoritative source, and compile a check-list, which you can tick off during your observations. Such a list cannot provide a complete picture of what a child is doing with talk. It is what the child does and says that will provide you with the information upon which you can most reliably base your comments.

It follows from this that the more opportunities a child is given to 'do and say', the greater will be your ability to note what is being achieved.

It follows also that, the more opportunities you can create for yourself to listen, watch, note, record, discuss with the child, the better is the chance you have of arriving at a fair and informative appraisal of a child's speaking and listening.

When you set out to collect information about children's speaking and listening, you will have in your head, or perhaps on a prompt-sheet of some kind to begin with, some ideas about the kinds of talk activity that are important for learning. This will not be a check-list, since you won't be using it to tick off each one when 'done', but it will help to inform the notes and comments you wish to make, without becoming so prescriptive that you fail to notice other significant qualities in the talk that is taking place. Among the things you will wish to consider are:

– What part children play in discussions
    focusing on what they need to know;
    responding to the ideas of others;
    giving space and listening to what others have to say;
    initiating discussion and sustaining it;
    summarising the discussion.
– How children give and follow instructions and share information.
– How children use talk to work their way towards a clearer understanding.
– What children show about their knowledge of and competence in language itself.
– How children adjust their talk for the person they are talking to and for other aspects of the situation they are in – e.g. formal situations, like presentations.
– The quality of the content of children's talk.

It is, however, worth remembering that:

• Assessment has a formative purpose at least as important as any summative one; it is as much a means of evaluating the nature and quality of the learning experience as it is of the learning itself.
• The children can be valuable participants in the evaluation of their own learning.
• Speaking and listening are interrelated activities, and a child's qualities as a listener should be an important focus for your observations.
• Talk is heavily dependent upon context. The situation in which talk takes place determines what talk takes place, and how much of it. Any assessment would therefore need to cover a variety of contexts as well as a number of occasions.
• Assessment is concerned with process as much as product. Ways in which children use exploratory, tentative talk, are therefore as significant as the use of more formal, presentational talk.
• Assessment has a vital diagnostic purpose, helping a teacher to identify where a child needs help and support.

Analysis

I finish this chapter with a very practical piece of work on assessing children's speaking and listening. It comes from the work of the National Oracy Project (NOP), a very influential group that published this piece in the early 1990s. As a result of its influence, the advice they offer is now rather typical of a great deal of practical guidance on the assessment of talk. I want you to read it alongside the work of Mercer (2000), who provides important theoretical connections with this form of practice.

Talk, as part of a literacy, is social and is guided by the cultural surroundings within which it occurs (Mercer, 2000). Assessing it only in school in terms of the talk which is encouraged there opens a socio-cultural 'can of worms'. What I feel is useful about the advice given by the NOP is their suggestion that teachers should look for as many different opportunities to observe talk as possible. Our behaviour will be influenced by our surroundings. For example, children who are quiet in the classroom can be extra-vert in the playground; those who are boisterous in the classroom may be more considered with their language at home or in another context. The classroom environment will not necessarily bring forth typical examples of talk. Just as Hilton wanted more and different forms of information about Stephen's reading earlier in this chapter (in the extract from Hall, 2003), teachers will need to examine various contexts and environments to really understand how effectively children can use talk.

Another positive feature about the NOP's (1991, p58) advice on assessing children's talk is to prompt teachers to study: *how the children use talk to work their way towards a clearer understanding*. Here, the writers acknowledge that talk aids learning and they want teachers to look for this in the children in their charge. They use the term 'exploratory talk' to identify the oracy that collaboratively solves problems and constructs new knowledge. Neil Mercer's (2000) work on encouraging exploratory talk is relevant here. He defines it as:

> that in which partners engage critically but constructively with each other's ideas. Relevant information is offered for joint consideration. Proposals may be challenged and counter-challenged, but if so, reasons are given and alternatives offered. Agreement is sought as a basis for joint progress. Knowledge is made publicly accountable and reasoning is visible in talk. (Mercer, 2000, p98)

Mercer rates this form of talk very highly as an effective form of talk among learners. For him, it models how participants in a conversation strive in a committed and unselfish manner to arrive at the best solutions. His view is that teachers need to provide the environments and the guidance to nurture this kind of talk.

Lastly, the NOP's question, 'How do I know what talk is better than other talk?', is an important area to discuss. It is partly related to the effective dialogues identified above, but it is also social and political. The way we talk indicates the regional and social position from which we come (Wood, 1988). Those listening to talk will come to conclusions very quickly in terms of power from the dialect that is used. The term 'dialect' refers to a language variety that has a distinctive grammar and vocabulary (Mallett, 2002). One can identify speakers as coming from a particular region of the country or from a particular social group through listening to the dialect. The National Curriculum English orders and the National Primary Strategy require teachers to teach children to speak in a particular form – Standard English. This dialect has acquired a special status through history and is associated with power. The reasons given for needing to teach this dialect are twofold: firstly, it is thought desirable to equip children with the means to talk in a way that suggests a high status; and secondly, it will enable larger groups of people to understand us – a *standard* form of English. Yet, as Wood (1988, p92) declares: *No one dialect of English, in any linguistic sense, is superior as a means of communication to any other. Although dialects vary in pronun-*

ciation and grammatical structures they are no less grammatical than Standard English. Therefore, the fact that one way of speaking is viewed as superior, more intelligent or more 'proper' than another way is not a linguistic phenomenon at all, but a political and social perspective (Wood, 1988). This view rejects the idea that children are somehow linguistically impoverished if they do not speak Standard English.

There are, of course, views to the contrary (Honey, 1997) which you will need to consider too. But if taken as true, this perspective leads to implications about how we teach children a dialect other than the one from home. It means teachers will need to discuss the correlation between power and language to avoid presenting children's home dialect as being deficient or lesser. I'm reminded here about O'Neil's (1970) conception of 'improper literacy' in the first chapter of this book. By negating children's primary literacy experiences, a process of disempowerment begins. It will also mean that assessment of children's talk has to draw on a holistic understanding of children's oral language to be in any way real and meaningful.

Once again, it would seem that there are no areas of the teaching of literacy that avoid controversy. However, by revealing the problems that exist in what we do, I hope you see how imperative it is to be well informed on the issues that have been raised and consequently how you choose to teach.

Personal response

- Which dialect do you use? Do you use one that has a privileged place in the curriculum and in the wider society? Have you ever felt you need to work at changing your dialect?
- Discuss these issues with a colleague. What is an accent? Can you speak in Standard English with an accent?
- When watching television, listen for different dialects. Who uses them on and when?

Practical implications and activities

Discuss with a teacher the merits of 'correcting' children's spoken grammar in the classroom. What will it achieve?

Observe children talking in the classroom setting – perhaps the role-play area – and listen for different dialects. Observe how the children are able to manipulate the language they use in role.

Writing activity

Choose a piece of writing from your journal, or another piece that you have written over the period of your course, and work on it to make it ready for publication on the web.

Further reading

Honey, J (1997) *Language and power: The story of Standard English and its enemies.* London: Faber & Faber

Wood, D (1988) *How children think and learn.* Oxford: Blackwell

References

Bakhurst, D and Shanker, S (eds) (2001) *Jerome Bruner: Language, culture, self.* London: Sage

Barrs, M and Browne, A (eds) (1991) *The reading book.* London: Centre for Literacy in Primary Education

Barrs, M and Cork, V (2001) *The reader in the writer: The links between the study of literature and writing development at Key Stage 2.* London: Centre for Literacy in Primary Education

Barrs, M and Ellis, S (1998) *The core booklist: A booklet to accompany 'the core book'.* London: Centre for Literacy in Primary Education

Barrs, M and Rosen, M (eds) (1997) *A year with poetry.* London: Centre for Literacy in Primary Education

Bates, E (1979) *The emergence of symbols.* New York: Academic Press

Bearne, E (2002) *Making progress in writing.* London: RoutledgeFalmer

Bearne, E (2003) 'Playing with possibilities: Children's multidimensional texts', in Bearne, E, Dombey, H and Grainger, T (eds) *Classroom interactions in literacy.* Maidenhead: Open University Press

Bearne, E, Dombey, H and Grainger, T (eds) (2003) *Classroom interactions in literacy.* Maidenhead: Open University Press

Benton, M (1978) 'Children's response to the text'. *4th Symposium of International Research Society*

Benton, M and Fox, G (1985) *Teaching literature: Nine to fourteen.* Oxford: Oxford University Press

Booth, D and Neelands, J (eds) (1998) *Writing in role, classroom projects connecting writing and drama.* Hamilton, Ontario: Caliburn Enterprises

Brice-Heath, S (1983) *Ways with words: Language, life, and work in communities and classrooms.* Cambridge: Cambridge University Press

Bruner, J S (1960) *The process of education.* Cambridge, MA: Harvard University Press

Bruner, J S (1972) *The relevance of education.* Harmondsworth: Penguin Education

Bruner, J S (1983) *Child's talk: Learning to use language.* Oxford: Oxford University Press

Bruner, J S (1996) *The culture of education.* Cambridge MA: Harvard University Press

Calderhead, J (1994) 'Teaching as a professional activity', in Pollard, A and Bourne, J (eds) *Teaching and learning in the primary school.* London: Routledge

Coles, G (2000) *Misreading reading: The bad science that hurts children.* Portsmouth, NH: Heinemann

Cordon, R (2000) *Literacy and learning through talk: Strategies for the primary classroom.* Buckingham: Open University Press

Cremin, M and Grainger, T (2001) *Resourcing drama in the primary classroom 8-14*. Loughborough: NATE

Crystal, D (1998) *Language play*. London: Penguin

D'Arcy, P (1999) *Two contrasting paradigms for the teaching and the assessment of writing: A critique of current approaches in the NC*. Loughborough: NATE

Department of Education and Science (1989) *English for ages 5-16*. London: DES

Department for Education and Employment (1998) *The National Literacy Strategy: Framework for teaching*. London: DfEE

DfEE (1999) *National Curriculum Attainment Targets for English Key Stage 1 and 2*. London: DfEE

Department for Education and Employment (2000) *Progression in phonics*. London: DfEE

Department for Education and Employment (2003) *Speaking, listening and learning handbook*. London: DfEE

Dias, P and Hayhoe, M (1988) *Developing response to poetry*. Milton Keynes: Open University Press

Dombey, H (1999) 'Towards a balanced approach to phonics teaching'. *Reading*, 33(2), July. United Kingdom Reading Association

Dombey, H and Moustafa, M (eds) (1998) *Whole to part phonics: How children learn to read and spell*. London: Centre for Literacy in Primary Education

Foster, J (ed) (1998) *School's out: poems about school*. Oxford: Oxford University Press.

Fox, C (1993) *At the very edge of the forest: The influence of literature on storytelling by children*. London: Cassell

Frater, G (2000) 'Observed in practice, English in the National Literacy Strategy: Some reflections'. *Reading* 34(3), November

Freebody, P (1992) 'A socio-cultural approach: Resourcing four roles as a literacy learner', in Watson, A and Badenhop, A (eds) *Prevention of reading failure*. Sydney: Scholastic

Gee, J P (2004) *Situated language and learning: A critique of traditional schooling*. London: Routledge

Geekie, P, Cambourne, B and Fitzsimmons, P (1999) *Understanding literacy development*. London: Trentham

Goodman, K (ed) (1973) *Miscue analysis: Applications to reading instruction*. Urbana, IL: ERIC/NCTE

Goodman, K (1986) *What's whole on whole language?* London: Scholastic

Goodwin, P (1999) 'The literate classroom: An introduction', in Goodwin, P (ed) *The literate classroom*. London: David Fulton

Goodwin, P (ed) (2001) *The articulate classroom: Talking and learning in the primary classroom*. London: David Fulton

Graham, J and Kelly, A (2000) *Reading under control: Teaching reading in the primary school* (2nd edition). London: David Fulton

Graham, L and Johnson, A (2003) *Children's writing journals*. Royston: United Kingdom Literacy Association

Grainger, T (1997) *Traditional storytelling in the primary classroom.* London: Scholastic

Grainger, T and Cremin, M (2001) *Resourcing drama in the primary classroom 5-7.* Loughborough: NATE

Grainger, T and Tod, J (2000) *Inclusive educational practice: Literacy.* London: David Fulton

Grainger, T, Goouch, K and Lambirth, A (2005a) *Creative activities for plot character and setting ages 5-7.* London: Scholastic

Grainger, T, Goouch, K and Lambirth, A (2005b) *Creative activities for plot character and setting ages 7-9.* London: Scholastic

Grainger, T, Goouch, K and Lambirth, A (2005c) *Creative activities for plot character and setting ages 9-11.* London: Scholastic

Grainger, T, Goouch, K and Lambirth, A (2005d) *Creativity and writing: Developing voice and verve in the classroom.* London: Routledge

Graves, D (1983) *Writing: Teachers and children at work.* Portsmouth, NH: Heinemann

Grugeon, E, Hubbard, L, Smith, C and Dawes, L (1999) *Teaching speaking and listening in the primary school* (2nd edition). London: David Fulton

Hall, K (2003) *Listening to Stephen read: Multiple perspectives on literacy.* Buckingham: Open University Press

Hannon, P (2000) *Reflecting on literacy education.* London: RoutledgeFalmer

Harrison, C (1999) 'When scientists don't agree: The case for balanced phonics'. *Reading*, 33(2), July

Honey, J (1997) *Language and power: The story of Standard English and its enemies.* London: Faber & Faber

Iser, W (1978) *The act of reading.* London: Routledge

Jones, K (2003) *Education in Britain: 1944 to the present day.* Oxford: Polity Press

Kress, G (1997) *Before writing: Rethinking the paths to literacy.* London: Routledge

Lambirth, A (2002) *Poetry matters.* Royston: United Kingdom Literacy Association

Lambirth, A (ed) (2005) *Planning creative literacy lessons.* London: David Fulton

Lankshear, C and Knobel, M (2003) *New literacies: Changing knowledge and classroom learning.* Buckingham: Open University Press

Mallett, M (2002) *The primary English encyclopaedia: The heart of the curriculum.* London: David Fulton

Marsh, J (2005) 'Introduction: Children of the digital age', in Marsh, J (ed) *Popular culture, new media and digital literacy in early childhood.* London: RoutledgeFalmer

Marsh, J and Millard, E (2000) *Literacy and popular culture: Using children's culture in the classroom.* London: Paul Chapman

Mayher, J, Lester, N and Pradl, G (1983) *Learning to write/writing to learn.* Upper Montclair, NJ: Boynton/Cook

McGuinness, D (1998) *Why children can't read and what we can do about it.* London: Penguin

McNaughton, M J (1997) 'Drama and children's writing: A study of the influence of drama on imaginative writing of primary school children'. *Research in Drama Education,* 2(1)

Medwell, J, Wray, D, Poulson, L and Fox, R (1998) *Effective teachers of literacy: A report of a research project commissioned by the Teacher Training Agency.* Exeter: Exeter University

Meek, M (1991) *On being literate.* London: Bodley Head

Mercer, N (2000) *Words and minds: How we use language to think together.* London: Routledge

Merchant, G and Thomas, H (1999) *Picture books for the literacy hour: Activities for primary teachers.* London: David Fulton

Miskin, R (1998) *Best practice phonics.* London: Heinemann

Mroz, M, Smith, F and Hardman, F (2000) 'The discourse of the literacy hour'. *Cambridge Journal of Education,* 30(3)

National Oracy Project (1991) *Teaching, talking and learning in Key Stage 2.* York: National Curriculum Council

O'Brian, V (1985) *Teaching poetry in the secondary school.* London: Arnold

Office for Standards in Education (1993) *Boys and English.* London: DES

Office for Standards in Education (2005) *The National Literacy and Numeracy Strategies and the Primary Curriculum.* London: OFSTED

Olson, D (1996) *The world on paper: The conceptual and cognitive implications of writing and reading.* Cambridge: Cambridge University Press

Olson, D (2001) 'Education: The bridge from culture to mind', in Bakhurst, D and Shanker, S G (eds) *Jerome Bruner: Language, culture, self.* London: Sage

O'Neil, W (1970) Properly literate. *Harvard Educational Review,* 40(2)

O'Neill, C (1995) *Drama worlds: A framework for process drama.* Portsmouth, NH: Heinemann

Pelligrini, A D (1984) 'The effects of dramatic play on children's generation of cohesive texts'. *Discourse Processes,* 7: 57–67

Pinker, S (1994) *The language instinct: How the mind creates language.* New York: William Marrow

QCA (1998) *Can do better – Raising boys' achievement in English.* London: QCA

Rosen, M (1989) *Did I hear you write?* (2nd edition). Nottingham: Five Leaves

Rumelhart, D (1976) 'Toward an interactive model of reading'. Technical Report No. 56. San Diego Centre for Human Information Processing, University of California

Sarland, C (1982) *The child and the book: A critical exploration with cultural implications.* MA thesis: Institute of Education

Scholes, R (1985) *Textual power: Literary theory and the teaching of English.* London: Yale University Press

Sedgwick, F (1997) *Read my mind: Young children, poetry and learning.* London: Routledge

Smith, F (1978) *Reading.* Cambridge: Cambridge University Press

Smith, F (1982) *Writing and the writer.* London: Heinemann

Solar, J, Wearmouth, J and Reid, G (eds) (2002) *Contextualising difficulties in literacy development: Exploring politics, culture, ethnicity and ethics.* London: RoutledgeFalmer

Vygotsky, L (1978a) *Thought and language.* Cambridge, MA: MIT Press

Vygotsky, L (1978b) *Mind in society: The development of higher psychological processes.* Cambridge, MA: Harvard University Press

Watson, J and Johnston, R (1998) 'Accelerating reading attainment: The effectiveness of synthetic phonics'. *Interchange* (57), Edinburgh: Scottish Office

Wells, G (1981) *Learning through interaction: The study of language development.* Cambridge: Cambridge University Press

Wilson, A with Hughes, S (eds) (1998) *The poetry book for primary schools.* London: Poetry Society

Wood, D (1988) *How children think and learn.* Oxford: Blackwell

Index